The Senior Partner

David E Cochrane
MSc; MSc; Cert Ed.
07532 066 440
Law066440@gmail.com
Eurowills.com
Writes as Edd King
Find him on Amazon Books

The Senior Partner

The Senior Partner

Edd King

September 2022

The right of Edd King to be identified as the Author of this work has been asserted by him in accordance with the Copyright, Design and Patents Act 1988 and any amendments thereto or renactments thereof in so far as they enhance or preserve the Author's rights. All rights reserved. All names used in this book are fictional and made up by the author. No offence is intended and if they happen to be real people it is purely accidental. No part of this publication may be reproduced stored in a retrieval system or transmitted in any form or by any means without the prior written permission of the Author or his Agents or be otherwise circulated in any form of binding or cover other than that in which it is published and without a similar condition being imposed on any subsequent purchaser.

Copyright © Edd King 2022

Author's note.

An alternative title for this book could well be '**Broken Justice**', an account of the failings of the UK criminal justice system [CJS] where decent, law-abiding people are convicted of offences and often sent to prison. These cases highlight failings; the police not investigating a crime but taking at face-value accusations made by the complainant; of the solicitors involved who fail to understand the nature of the alleged crimes and often wrongly advise a defendant to plead guilty to receive a lesser sentence; of the criminal barristers usually all self-employed who are miserably recompensed by the legal aid fund and who are understandably keen to move on to their next and perhaps more lucrative assignment, and so fail to prepare for a trial in many cases having received a brief the day before trial. Or are just incompetent; the crown prosecution service lawyers who often do not bother to question the evidence and miss the obvious or where the very wording of the charges demanded further investigation; an accuser who has an ulterior motive in pursuing the accused and over-stating the case by fabrication or non-disclosure of evidence helpful to the defence; and the grooming of witnesses; then the Criminal Cases Review Commission, grossly underfunded and whose limited powers leave many people wrongly convicted and unable to obtain redress, and who deal with one or two percent only of the cases referred to them; delays in getting a case heard which means genuinely innocent persons suffering added mental anguish at not having their day in court sometimes for years, unable to keep his job or find new employment. Then the issues with the adversarial system where the best-prepared side wins, not because of guilt or innocence necessarily but the experience and preparedness or otherwise of the barristers involved. And another issue I'd like to raise; an assumed guilt just because a defendant chooses not to give evidence.

The narrative which follows is a damning indictment of a system now in turmoil, a situation that has been brewing over years and now needs urgent attention to right the wrongs of the past, to compensate those wrongly convicted and to ensure the CJS operates fairly in the future. I have not used the real names or places where the subject worked, but the issues are real and the persons involved may well recognise themselves but I have chosen not to identify them here. I have however recounted the facts as well as my memory served me aided by comprehensive notes and study of the evidence all of which should have been done years ago by everyone involved in the case and which indicates to me a real situation where my character should not have been convicted or even have gone to trial and has since done a great deal on his own in an attempt to overturn the conviction.

To illustrate the enormity of the wrongful conviction issue I have referred to learned authors' texts and which, on reading, have convinced me even more of the problem, much of which never enters the public domain; in short, the UK CJS just does not want to know, does not want to have dragged into the open and aired *coram populo* for fear of the outrage it will engender. Hopefully this missive will incite someone or some group of people to use this little book as an example of just how fragile is the public's notion that the CJS is in good health. And to help my subject, John Cairns*

*Not his real name.

It is relevant here to quote Peter Joyce, QC, of Nottingham, in his letter to The Times 31 July 2021.

> *Sir. Your article [Law July 29] about the shortage of criminal law barristers comes as no surprise to any criminal practitioners nor can it surprise the holders of the office of justice secretary or lord chief justice over the past 25 years. The criminal bar has for years been warning those in power and authority that they risk destroying what Sir Bill Jeffrey in his review in 2014 described as a precious national asset. He also warned that once lost it would be almost impossible to reclaim. The police, legal aid, probation service, courts and both branches of the legal profession [in short the entire criminal justice system] have all been deliberately underfunded by successive governments. A properly funded criminal justice system is the bedrock of a civilised society. Ours used to be the envy of the world and copied by many. Now it is broken and is probably beyond repair. No doubt as always, the ministry of Justice will blandly claim that 'all is well' and continue paying the ukulele as the ship finally sinks. Peter Joyce, QC, Nottingham*

And an article by Jonathan James, Legal editor of The Times. Friday August 5th 2022.

> *A legal watchdog is to review whether appealing against alleged miscarriages of justice is too difficult because the test which judges use is overly harsh. Ministers have told the Law Commission, which advises on legislative reform*

in England and Wales, to report on claims that miscarriages cases struggle to get before the Court of Appeal. Last year a report from a cross-party parliamentary group on miscarriages of justice found that the test 'acts as a brake' on the body that refers cases to the court.

Under the test, the court must decide whether a disputed conviction is unsafe. The authors of the Westminster Commission on Miscarriages of Justice pointed out that the test contrasts with the position around appeals of sentence where the issue is whether the sentence was 'manifestly excessive or wrong in principle'.

Cases involving allegations of miscarriages of justice must first be taken to the Criminal Cases Review Commission [CCRC] created in 1997 and which heard claims in England and Wales and Northern Island. In its report the Westminster Commission, which was co-chaired by Lord Garnier QC, a former Conservative solicitor-general, recommended the creation of a more objective test by which the Commission would refer cases where 'convictions may be unsafe, the sentence may be excessive or wrong in law or that it is in the interest of justice'.

According to the authors, such a reform 'would encourage a different and more independent mindset'. In its announcement yesterday, the Law Commission said it would report on whether there was evidence that the existing test used to grant an appeal against a conviction *on the grounds that it is unsafe 'may make it difficult to correct any miscarriages of justice'. A spokesman for the Commission said no specific case had triggered the review, but that the Commissioners were reacting to the cross-party report and similar concerns railed by the commons justice committee.*

The Commission said it would also review the attorney-general's powers to refer cases to the court where there were concerns that a sentence was 'unduly lenient' as well as laws governing the retention and disclosure of evidence for a case, including after conviction, and retention and access to records of proceedings. Commenting on the review, which could take up to two years to compete, Professor Penny Lewis, the Commissioner for criminal law, said that 'the appeals system had faced calls for reform in recent years, often marked by conflicting views on the areas of law that should be changed'. She said the review would 'scrutinise where the law is working well, and where it may be falling short', adding 'It's essential that there is clarity, efficiency and fairness in criminal appeals at all levels.'

Helen Pitcher, chairwoman of the CCRC, welcomed the review, saying that her organisation had called for analysis of the appeals process 'for a number of years'. Garnier's' report contained a brutal assessment of the CCRC, arguing that it suffered from budget cuts, increased workloads, and even alleged interference from the Ministry of Justice. Yesterday Pitcher said that the CCRC was 'committed to finding and investigating miscarriages of justice and it is right that the appeals system is regularly and robustly scrutinised.'

Look at the first few pages of Michael Naughton's 'Wrongful convictions: towards a zemiological analysis of the tradition of criminal justice system reform'.

> *In the history of England and Wales' Criminal Justice System (CJS) a discernible tradition of CJS reform emerges that exhibits the following discursive rules. At particular times, particular wrongful conviction cases are debated. In these debates, these particular cases attain a high profile 'miscarriage' status that throws the government, legal and public/media spheres into chaotic collision. As a result, legislative reforms have to be introduced to the CJS that serve to resolve the situation whereupon normality between and within the colliding spheres can, at least, be temporarily resumed.*
>
> *Within this discernible tradition, this article applies ideas derived from zemiology (the science/study of societal harm - social, physical, psychological and financial) and focuses upon some of the broader consequences of wrongful criminal convictions and/or miscarriages of the CJS. In particular, the article attempts to emphasise: the routine, as opposed to the exceptional, nature of miscarriages of the CJS; the zemiological costs of these to both the victims and to the public; the way that recognition of the above is obscured beneath the publicity that surrounds exceptional cases; and the failure of governments to act except in times of extreme*

public pressure, when knowledge of these is evident in the published statistics available.

It is concluded that the scale of the wrongful criminal conviction phenomenon demonstrates a reductive approach to punishment that cannot be regarded as attributable to mere error, anomaly, or even systemic malpractice. On the contrary, the extent of the problem intimates a purposeful complacency and failure to act by both the government and the agencies that comprise the CJS, except in times of extreme pressure and perceived public crisis. From a zemiological perspective, this complacency and failure to act entails profound consequences, which fundamentally calls into question the continued legitimacy of current criminal conviction practices.

That notion is that we in the UK have what is regarded as the fairest CJS in the world, but cases, recent and old, drive a coach and horses through that belief. The justice system in the United States is bad, we all know that, but the UK is catching up fast. Much of what you will read here is difficult to believe; how could this happen? Read on and find out.

PART ONE – JOHN CAIRNS

It all began with an email to one of my many accounts, but this one was to the address I used in my works as a writer, MODUK and one I rarely checked. It was obviously from somebody I knew - or somebody who knew me. It was signed off 'JC' but his e-address gave away his true identity, John Cairns. I knew the guy from years back. I replied adding my 'phone number.

Cairns and I had worked together in the Forces many years ago. He was a real tough guy, volunteering for all the dodgy jobs which usually meant that I and a few others got involved in helping him get into the ops area wherever that might have been, and out again safely. Yeah, it was fun and sometimes bloody dangerous, but that was what we had signed up for and were paid to do. The main problem with Cairns was that he was highly intelligent. I was told that he had left the Army after obtaining an OU degree in some subject or other and had got a job doing something somewhere in London. And that was all I knew. I never saw him after I left and he never attended any of the few reunions I actually went to as he, like most of us, never really wanted to talk about the old days and in particular, not come face to face with guys who I knew when they were barely into their mid-twenties, and were now well past retirement age, and many of them looking it too. Frankly it was depressing as I no doubt looked the same to them. That was Cairns all over. He never told anybody about his Army job, but I know he made it to Major, the highest commissioned rank he could then attain after being in the ranks. There were quite a few things about a service career which really bugged me and that was one of them.   I did not forget the guy, but was a bit surprised that he didn't reply straight away. I just assumed he was busy, but at age seventy plus he would surely be retired. It took him two weeks to get back to me. He called.

"Where are you living now, Edd?"

"Oxford. You?"

"Southampton."

"You want to meet?"

"Not really. But I need to see you." Alarm bells started ringing.

"You have some kind of problem?" There was a long pause. Cairns was not a guy to show emotion or ever be without a solution to any issues which needed dealing with.

"Yeah, mate, like you wouldn't know."

"Okay, I'll pay for the beers, right?"

"Come down here. I'll email my address. Stay over for a couple of days. It may take some time." Now I was worried.

"Of course. When."

"To suit you. I've got time. You have other things to do so …"

"I'll make time. Send me some dates."

"Yeah. Will do. Cheers." Now I was more than just worried. This was not the old Cairns I knew. His prob sounded like it was serious.

Cairn's address, in a block of flats in Southampton, turned out to be a new block facing over the marina. I called him when the satnav dumped me outside the entrance to the garage. Cairns took only a minute to appear standing inside the building as the garage door rolled up. He beckoned me in. He still looked like a man you would not want to get too close to when he was using an ATM. He had put on a bit of weight his hair was streaked with silver but he didn't move like a man of seventy three. He slipped into the passenger seat of my little car.

"Up a floor. Bay number thirty-eight. How are you mate?" The guy looked straight ahead while he spoke, like he was busy looking for threats, potential targets, in the gloom of the garage. Old habits die hard.

"Yeah, great." I found the bay and turned in. "Now we take the lift." I grabbed my overnight bag from the boot and followed my host to the lift. I made a note to look at the details the land-registry held on the property. It was just something I did. Then the lift moved up two floors.

"Good trip?"

"Yeah. You married, didn't you?"

"Yeah. She's got her own place now. She still works."

"Kids?"

The Senior Partner

"Yeah. Three. All got good jobs. All left home. You?"

"Yeah. Three." The small talk stopped when the lift reached the third floor. I followed him out, turning left then onto a large patio planted with shrubs and trees. Very nice. He opened the door to his flat and he stood aside to let me in first. I made for the large picture-window which overlooked the marina.

"Coffee?" He called from the kitchenette.

"Please. White no sugar."

"You got it." It was as if we were still working together. He put the kettle on and picked my suitcase off the settee where I had left it. "I'll put this in your room." I followed him. He put me in the master bedroom, with en-suite. The sun streamed in the window, and below it painted a thick, glossy bright silver stream across the marina. I liked it. I took off my jacket and chucked it onto the bed. Cairns was back in the kitchen. He had rattan chairs and table on his veranda where he had placed the coffees and a packet of McVitie's original plain digestive biscuits. My impression was that he was very restrained. Not like the ebullient Cairns I knew. Something was wrong. He slid onto the veranda, picked up his coffee cradled it in both hands, sat down and leaned back in his chair. He looked at me and smiled. "Well, Edd, you ain't fat or bald but probably stinking rich, being a writer. To answer your question. It was your book, Nelson's Law that I read. I liked it. If it was meant to be a bio, it was all bloody lies! So, what did you do when you handed back your kit to the MOD?" I dunked another digestive, careful not to allow it to get too soggy and drop into my coffee, shoved it whole into my mouth, and looked out over the yachts and motor cruisers jigging around each other as they made for their moorings or for the open sea. I just wondered how many of them engaged in some kind of smuggling and how many skippers had bribed an easy passage through immigration and customs. I was slipping back into the old job again. Once in, never out. It was the Cairns getting at me. He spoke before I had swallowed the soggy biscuit.

"Can't tell you that, mate 'cos I did so much. You?"

"I went into the law." Then I shifted my gaze to him.

"You were a cop?"

"Hell, no! Worse than that!"

"Really? What could be worse that being a cop?"

"What about estate agents?"

"Try lawyers!"

"You a lawyer? So that Nelson's Law story was true?" I laughed.

"Yes. But a lot of it wasn't!"

"So, did you get that girl at the end of the book or not?"

"That's something er …I cannot answer that question. My name is King. My rank is … was … colonel and my number is ……" Cairns laughed. He had loosened up.

"I bet you did you bastard! Hey, I liked that! So, you still working as a lawyer?"

"No, thank Christ! Biggest mistake of my life! What about you?" He became serious again.

"Me?" He swivelled round in his chair, throwing his right leg over his left, so he was no longer facing me but gazing out to sea. I felt his mood change. He did not want to look at me as he told me about something that was weighing on his mind.

"Yeah, really, Edd, I was a lawyer. Got my degree when I was at Colchester. Then spent the last two years or so of my service doing the Legal Practice Course. The MoD let me do that, and I actually enjoyed it. Mainly being able to relax away from all the Army bullshit, and not dropping to the deck whenever a bloody door slammed or a car backfired. You know the score!"

"No. I don't. I wasn't involved in all that crap which never gets into the papers but crosses the desks of those MI6 buggers. You, mate, are lucky to be alive, especially after Soxmis! Those guys would shoot if you so much as looked at them!"

"Don't go there, Edd. You did your bit as well. Anyway, yeah, did the LPC and got articles with a local firm started on the day I left. I lived in my own house, one of two I had bought. I tell you something, mate. It was a pleasant change from my seventeen years in the Army." He emptied his coffee cup.

"My articles were crap."

"So were mine. I was on twenty quid a week. Worked with a legal exec who only spent half his time in the office. I spent most of mine sitting in on cases. Holding the barristers' hands and marvelling at just how badly prepared they were. I never had any instruction on anything. The receptionist there Sharon, was a right pain. Wore far too much makeup, and treated me like a tea-boy. I was always running errands for the boss, and I don't know how many times I had to go to the Old Bailey for a day just waiting to get a court, then back the next day, same thing. All for fifteen quid an hour waiting time. Which of course went to the firm, not to me!"

"Yeah, been there done that. Anyway, why am I here now? I don't think it's to chew the cud." The guy kept looking out to sea, where I could not see his face as he spoke. For about fifteen seconds he said nothing.

"No, it ain't, Edd. It's not to chew the cud. It's because of my last job. Some bastard accused me of nicking nearly a hundred thousand quid and got me jailed." Cairns stood up and left the veranda, and I heard a door slam. I could have sworn that he was crying. I did not follow him. Nor did I believe that John had stolen any money, but I did know that the guy wanted help and I was determined to assist him.

I suspected too that John had read my book on criminology and had an idea that I could help him. I recall the notes I made regarding wrongful convictions while writing that book it went something like this.

'Are you one of the many thousands of people who feel they have been wrongfully convicted of a criminal offence? Do you feel that someone has fabricated or withheld evidence that should have been made available at the time? Was your lawyer overworked, underfunded and unable to do his job? Were you sure that your defence team were competent? Were you advised to plead guilty for an offence or offences you did not commit just because you were told you'd get a lighter sentence? If so, have you managed to have the conviction overturned or do you plan to try or have you tried and failed?

Many professionals engaged in the administration of justice feel that delay in bringing cases to court, together with incompetent solicitors and barristers and corrupt police officers or sloppy investigations too often results in a gross disservice to defendants in that they are convicted whilst in fact innocent or where due to careless investigations victims of crime do not see justice done. Where a person is wrongfully convicted, the consequences of the conviction can last a lifetime, and he finds for myriad reasons that fighting for justice can be lengthy, frustrating and expensive and in many cases he may never achieve satisfaction, and where he is genuinely innocent of any crime it, like a tattoo, remains with him forever.

The system of appeals is based on certain principles and procedures which do not, generally, allow for an argument challenging a case which, legal niceties aside, 'just does not add up'. A further hurdle is that after a certain period all documents relating to cases are destroyed. This is a disadvantage to any appellant, but should not mean that the case can never be revisited.

The Criminal Cases Review Commission is the public body responsible for investigating alleged miscarriages of justice. Under certain circumstances they send a case for a fresh appeal. They are independent of the police, the courts and the government. The CCRC has hitherto enjoyed a less then comfortable relationship with the appeal courts, but in view of the fact that the courts are having to deal with many more appeals against conviction and sentence, some accommodation must be made with the CCRC to ensure that where no paper-trail remains, new cogent argument should be allowed as the basis of an appeal.

In any event, where a person has served his sentence he cannot recover the time lost, but he may certainly recover his self-respect and maybe employment where he takes the time, trouble and suffers the heartache of raking over the ashes of his past to get the matter before the courts again. I believe that where an application is made in the light of 'exceptional circumstances', it should be looked upon favourably. By 'exceptional circumstances' I mean situations such as the one I have set out in this little book, as experienced by my good friend, John Cairns.

Consider the note by Jennifer Schmidt-Petersen, the Programme and Student Lead for Policing Programmes at ULaw;

"With crime documentaries like 'Making a Murderer' drawing in huge audiences across the world and searches for 'wrongful convictions in the UK' rising by a huge 84% in the last 12 months, there's clear interest in the UK justice system." I might add that it should be looked at as a matter of urgency.

I sat on the veranda deep on thought. I did not want to believe what John had just told me. But I had to believe him, and I resolved, again, to do all I could to help. I quietly went to the kitchenette and made myself another coffee and returned to my chair and the views across the marina. Then I worked on a plan. I needed to know the facts, all of them. I would ask John to send me a statement of the case, leaving nothing out, even anything he thought was of no importance including matters which he maybe thought could have caused any observer to suspect that he had been pocketing money he was not entitled to. Then I needed to know what he had done to try and get the case heard again. I must have sat there for over an hour before John reappeared. He dumped a bottle of lager onto the table and sat down.

"Sorry, mate."
"Don't be John." I put a hand on his arm. "I'm going to do all I can to help you get this looked at again. I know you wouldn't steal

anything. I'll work on it night and day." He reached for his beer, and I finished my coffee. "Where are your wife and kids?"

"Elaine used to be a secretary, now works as a midwife in Abberton. Lives in the Colchester house I bought years ago. My two lads are both working as engineers, and my daughter works for the BBC. In television. I did my articles in Chelmsford. When I qualified in eighty-two, I did a lot of locum work mainly so I could keep an eye on my various business interests. Did that for years until about eighty-eight. Then moved to a job in Alresford, where I owned a small bungalow. I sold all my businesses and all the stock and vehicles, because I had kids and wanted to live a more settled life."

I let John talk on. He was clearly relieved to be able to talk about his transfer from military to life as a civilian and his work as a GP lawyer. Then he touched on his last engagement where he found trouble. I interrupted his thoughts.

"Okay, John. Thanks for that. Now, what I want you to do is sit down sometime and commit all this to paper. Dates, names, places … what you did and what the other guy did. All of it. Don't be too worried. You ain't gonna write a doctoral thesis, I'll deal with tidying it all up, all the syntax. I think this exercise will enable you to just let it all come out. Anything that's in your head, I want it out. Can you do that for me?"

"Yeah, Edd, of course. I've written a lot of it anyway. Now lets call a halt. It's nearly dinner time. I know a nice little restaurant near here. Shanghai Bay. We can walk."

The meal was good. We had a couple of beers and walked back to the flat. Next morning, John was up early. I stuck my head into the kitchen where he was tucking into some porridge.

"Breakfast, Edd?"

"Na. I only eat once a day but I'll make myself some coffee. You off to work?"

"Yeah. I do loading of containers at the docks. Every time I sit on the bloody machines, I keep reminding myself. What the effin' hell am I doing this for? I'm a bloody lawyer! Should be earning ten times as much! Really pisses me off! But I'd rather work with those guys than any damn lawyers any day. They're all up-front, say what they mean, mean what they say. No bullshit legal-speak, 'I'm better than you' crap, just honest-to-goodness blokes. So, they probably never read a newspaper but they just get on with their jobs. Look, there's a spare key hanging on the hook here …" He pointed to the board by the fridge. "Lock up behind you and drop the key through the letterbox!" He spooned the last bits of porridge into his mouth. "Been great to see you again, Edd. I have every confidence in you. Take care."

Then he was gone. I had a shower, dressed and sunk a coffee. Then I packed and made it to the car. Oxford was only about ninety minutes' drive from the Southampton flat, but I was preoccupied with the problem John had thrown at me. I recalled Rawlings referring to the Criminal Cases Review Commission which over the past 20 years of its operation has found that seven percent of ten thousand cases it had studied represented wrongful convictions. That is seven hundred individuals convicted and maybe jailed for crimes they didn't commit. It appeared a routine feature of CJS operations. I decided to add the whole of the Rawlings paper as an annex to any report or paper I did for John. It makes for sobering reading.

Over the next two weeks, I could not get John's problem out of my mind, so I spent an inordinate amount of time looking up the issue of wrongful convictions and was truly shocked at what I found. Yes, it was bad in Australia, the States and some other countries there was just no real justice, Russia for one which in a so-called civilised country was just downright appalling. What kind of regime was that? It was equally bad if not worse in many other countries. But I was concerned only about the UK. In fact, recalling some of the trials I had been involved in with the barristers doing all the talking, how they had acted and the advice they had given the defendants was, in my view and with the benefit of hindsight, sometimes outrageous. And it dawned on me pretty quickly that the barristers who took up those magistrates' or Crown Court hearings were not the cream of the bunch. It was only in some 'high-profile' and privately funded cases where there was some improvement.

I was on the point of e-mailing John when I received a draft of his case. It was a long message. I added it to the folder I had opened as soon as I had returned from Southampton and which now held my own notes and a number of documents I had downloaded. There was a lot of them. I acknowledged the e-mail, then did an initial skip-through of the document. My first impressions were that John had been used by his senior partner and possibly by the firm's other partners as well. There was also an element of abuse and judging by the senior partner's behaviour, some psychological pressure as well. Overall, I thought John had been very badly treated but I understood his reasons for sticking with it. The reading also angered me. I knew there was a lot of bullying in the legal profession, and pressure on junior staff but the extent of what was done to John, by his account, took the biscuit. I emailed John again, telling him I was going to respond to his notes, para by para where I thought appropriate and maybe call him from time to time to discuss issues. That evening he responded. *'No pro. JC.'* I wanted to discuss with John any points which, if they occurred to me, might also occur to anybody reading the missive. And I wanted answers from him. John had clearly done a lot of work on this matter, and a lot of research and I just wondered how he could have put up with his tormentor, this senior partner, for so long as he appeared to be a most unpleasant character, and that John had been very patient, seemingly keen to make a go of his new job. His opening paragraphs were as follows, in this book edited for length.

John Cairn's submission.

'I am relating my experiences to my good friend and author Edd King. We followed similar careers; he also qualified as a lawyer after military service and it was through one of his books that I managed to contact him again. The issues I wanted to discuss with him were, what made the senior partner of small firm of solicitors target me so relentlessly and fabricate evidence against me that ended up by my going to jail? How did my defence team fail to ask the obvious questions or apply for documents which would have exonerated me? How did the CPS allow a period of three and a half years to elapse before the matter got to court? This is my story.

The Beginnings.

Children of serving military personnel may be forced to move home every three or so years and although it may give them an interesting life of travel and new challenges, it does not give them the best start in life educationally. At least that was the situation when I was born. I was a lively kid who loved the outdoors and once we moved to a semi-permanent home on the coast my sisters and I would ride our bikes for miles, swim in the sea, fish and sail our little dingy. It was our education which suffered most, but that was not anything I really worried about or then or even appreciated and I doubt very much if I would have cared even if I knew it. My non-outdoor passion was reading. We had no TV but we had radio and I read books whenever I could not get outside, and even at a young age I would regularly be top of the class in English and reading, and I was often asked to read out loud to my form, as I had what was then perceived to be an upper-class accent. However, it was when I attended what I knew would be my last school, my father now retired from HM forces, that I got a surprise. I was dumped into another school, new faces, new places new teachers again. Nowt new in that. But my first few lessons were so basic that I believed I was surrounded by the school dunces or so I thought, and so determined to do something about it. It was the kick up the backside I really needed. I worked hard and clawed my way into the [then] GCE stream and managed to obtain a couple of GCE passes. It was probably this shock realisation that if I didn't pull my socks up, I would leave school with no qualifications and be left behind in the jobs race. Thereafter, I turned my attention to the outside world and what I was going to do for the rest of my life. To bide time pending taking the big decisions, a little intro to 'work-ethics' would not go amiss, so I started work in a restaurant and as a paper-boy. I thought I might like to join the Army, so I visited the local Army recruiting asking for all the information about becoming joining-up. I read everything about what the army did. Next thing I knew, I was on the conveyor belt, and it all happened rather fast. Interviews went well, and in what seemed like no time, I was in uniform. After just a few years, I was somehow selected to undergo an officer training course and found myself at Sandhurst, wearing a pair of denims and with a good few others, being put through my paces, being constantly assessed and thoroughly enjoying myself. My training passed quickly and I did well, possibly something to do with an awakened [previously slumbering] competitiveness. I quickly categorised my fellow trainees as guys to steer clear of and the few others who seemed to apply themselves diligently to every aspect of the course. To cut a long story short, I spent about twenty years in the forces, my last tour was as a Major and, facing redundancy, I opted to leave and return to civvie street. My leaving date was about three years later, and in that time I studied law, and on my release date I started work as an articled clerk in Essex. Being shut up in an office after my previously diverse, interesting and mainly out-door life, was anathema to me and I thought I had probably made a big mistake, but I always endeavour to finish anything I start, so I stuck with it and was eventually admitted as a solicitor of the Supreme Court of Judicature of England and Wales. That was in the early eighties. Clearly, and despite a poor start educationally, I was able to work hard, organise and plan and make a reasonable success of my life to the benefit my family.

My period of articles was not overly beneficial and as our East London office had a good criminal practice run by a legal executive, I spent many hours sitting in on a number of Crown court trials including at the Central Criminal Court, the Old Bailey. It was after the first few days in the office that I felt very ill, and I put it down to the office environment. However, I was able to cover it up as I had to attend court and was able to leave the courtroom any time I wanted as Terry, my supervisor from the office, did not normally attend with me. It was then I thought that the office job was not really for me. Be that as it may, I soon sussed out that I was in fact being used as a 'gofer' so I asked my principal if I could move to the conveyancing department so I could actually learn something To give him his due, he engaged another clerk, Graham, who was not actually training to be a solicitor and was paid about two hundred and fifty quid per week for doing what I was paid twenty pounds for. I had also started a few businesses, and by the time I qualified I had a decent income from inter alia, a small property portfolio which I had started working on during my last years in the Service. I left my principal's firm when I qualified and by then had a very good working knowledge of conveyancing, having been aided by a very efficient secretary who was very friendly with many local estate agents and could audio type and carry on a conversation at the same time. Her telephone book listed her men-friends not by name but by what job they were able to do. After I was admitted to the Roll, I signed-up with a London law agency and worked as a locum conveyancing solicitor and all in all was kept pretty busy, but enjoying it. I made friends easily, as I am a very out-going person so meeting and dealing with people at all social levels was never a problem, and I believe that I gave my clients a good service. I did assignments all over the south of England, would occasionally stay in hotels but usually commuted from my main home.

Then I met Elaine, the girl who was to become my wife and within a year or so I was expecting my first child. Over the next six years, I cut back on business activities and bought a new property off-plan so our daughter could breathe fresh air and live a country life. My partner was keen to have a smallholding so we bought a few acres of land and applied for planning consent for a house. I took an employed position with a reasonably adjacent firm, and for a while was happy to knuckle-down and work, doing mainly residential and commercial conveyancing. However, the daily commute was a bit longer than I liked and inconvenient for my partner, so I contacted my old agency and asked if he could find an employed position closer to home. My agent soon found what appeared to be a couple of ideal positions, and I informed my current employer of my plans to move, and when I mentioned to their litigation partner the names of the two prospective employers he suggested that working for one of the options, which I shall call 'The Firm', would not be a good idea but he did not go into detail. That firm had three offices, and the one I would be working out of, if I took the job, could not have been better located geographically. I had done a quick recce. There was free parking, easy access to the town centre and it was only a few miles from my new property. The other, larger firm was known to me but it was not one I really wanted to work for. An interview was arranged and I duly attended their main office in a city centre, some hours' drive from home. The date was September 1988.

Meet The Firm.

The head office of my prospective employer turned out to be on the first-floor in a row of terraced properties, accessed off a busy pedestrian street, only a few hundred meters from the town's main thoroughfare and conveniently close to a multi-story car park and the courts. It was not a substantial business, but some substantial businesses are best avoided so that did not overly concern me. At the appointed hour I entered their offices which turned out to be arranged over four rooms and I was met by a receptionist who led me to their main office which overlooked the busy road from which I entered the building. There was a large table in my half-right position, at which sat two people, and a third person I now know as Donald Nichols, was standing with his back to the window. At the table were Charles Pope and the younger of the two was Fred Brooks. Nichols remained standing throughout the short interview. From the firm's title, Nichols and Pope, and from his age I assumed that Brooks was the junior partner.

NB *For the purpose of this exercise, the names are pseudonyms.*

I shook hands with all three. There was no discussion about my past employment or about my various disciplines in the law. The latter point would no doubt have been covered by my agency. The interview did not last very long. I was not offered any refreshment, there was no side banter about where I was living, or my family, or what I was doing before I moved into the law. It seemed a bit sanitised and the tenor of the interview was mainly about when I would be able to start, and some adverse comment about the other firm I had approached re. the new job and the comment by Nichols '*better to be a big fish in a small pond*'. In all, it was the most brief and shallow interview I had ever attended. Apart from these interventions by the senior partner, he seemed to take very little interest in the interview process. On reflection it appeared to be a shoo-in; subsequent events reinforced my impression. They wanted someone quickly and local knowledge, I discovered later, was that the firm had a poor reputation. With the formalities over, such as they were, I suggested that I might pop into the office I was to take over, if I were offered the post, to see the retiring fee-earner but, putting it mildly, this proposal was not well received. On reflection, that was the second hint that maybe things were not quite as I might have hoped they would be and frankly, had this firm not been so conveniently located and the first to interview me, I would not have worked for them. Not meeting the departing lawyer was not really a problem as I reasonably assumed that I would meet him /her when he / she handed over the files and briefed me on their current situation. Within a very few days, I was told that I had got the job. I informed my current employer and a start date was arranged. It was still the month of September when I entered the office at just after nine am.

The office was in what was once a private residence, accessed off a one-way street of terraced properties. At the lower end of the road was the town hall and the magistrates' court and at the upper end a church. Opposite the office was pedestrian access to the centre of the little market town. Of the rooms in the building, the firm occupied the lower-ground floor comprising a small street-side office which had no obvious function and a larger office at the back with a small kitchen area. The room gave views over a garden. On the ground floor there were two similar rooms, the smaller one was reception and secretarial with the larger room being the one I was to use as my office. There was a stairway leading to the upper floors and off the small landing half-way up was a toilet and a small wash-handbasin. The upper floor was occupied by another business.

The former employee had already left and I regretted not meeting him to do a formal hand-over. Not one of the partners Donald, Charles or Fred were there to see me in either. In fact, I never met or ever spoke to Fred again. There were two office staff to meet me, Sarah, a legal executive whom I came to respect as a person and as a brilliant family lawyer, and Denise, the secretary / typist. [*NB again pseudonyms*]. The office I was allocated had double doors leading to a small conservatory where a number of files were stored on the floor. In the office, there were two chairs, two filing cabinets but no books. On the desk there was a Dictaphone, a diary and a couple of files which were marked as 'work in progress'. In the diary there was a comment from the departing employee *'non hic beatus'* indicating some dissatisfaction with his [former] post, and doubtless keen to move to pastures new. NB; when he was later contacted to comment, he refused to become involved. Sarah and Denise were really helpful. Denise had been doing all the conveyancing work and proved to be very good at it. Sarah was a busy fee-earner who spent a lot of her time in court. I noted with some surprise that Denise only had an electric typewriter on which she did the conveyancing work and all Sarah's documents. The office décor was a bit tired. Overall, I was not ecstatic about the place.

I settled in, and after a briefing from Denise I worked my way through the current cases, preparing them for completion, checking that we had done all the searches and where appropriate had requisitioned the mortgage funds and drafted the completion statements. Then late morning, I received a 'phone call from Nichols telling me that there was an ongoing dispute with the local planning office, and would I deal with it. I was a bit concerned of course, as this was not really my brief, but I took it on board and dealt with it anyway. It related to the size of an advertising board which Nichols had fixed to an external wall adjacent to the front door of the building and according to the planning office Nichols had not even applied for permission to erect it. The next day I had to drive my partner to hospital for long-standing appointment but was back in the office by lunchtime. On my return, I was informed by Denise that Nichols was 'pissed off' about my taking the time off, and had apparently entered into some diatribe about married men and their family problems. Nobody from the head office called me to express their concern for my partner or at all. I just got on with my work. I had completions to deal with and the work was more important than bothering too much about the call from Nichols. Was I by now harbouring any doubts about the job? Yes, I was but I am not a quitter and there were still a few plusses as far as I was concerned. In addition, I noted that Denise was struggling to do all Sarah's work and the conveyancing work on an electric typewriter so I looked at the idea of getting a PC for her to use.

The next issue was more serious. The following day, late morning, I was visited by both Nichols and Pope who turned up at the office unannounced, which I suppose was their prerogative. It was lucky I was in. They opened with the usual questions such as how was I getting on. Then Nichols asked me if I would *'underquote how much we are paying you. Can you say eight instead of ten thousand pounds'*. I cannot now recall the exact sums, but I was rather taken aback for two reasons. Firstly, I was being asked to perpetrate a fraud, involve myself in a conspiracy to defraud, and secondly I doubted that the commission payable to the agency would be very much different at ten thousand as it would be for eight. This was not the first indication that maybe the firm's accounts were not overly heathy. Charlie Pope was suitably embarrassed by Nichols' request but he didn't then seem at all concerned by it. My response was that I had no intention of contacting the agent in any case as I never had on previous occasions. I did, however, take the opportunity to suggest to the partners that the office needed 'tidying up' and secondly, that we needed a PC for the work Denise was doing. My partner, a legal secretary of many years standing, had been using word processors for ages. On this last issue, I had speculatively approached the firm's usual supplier of office equipment and stationery to discuss the matter generally and then spoke to their rep when he had dropped in to introduce himself and take orders from Denise. He furnished me with some entirely unsolicited information from which I got the impression that the firm was not the best client the supplier had, hinting at payment problems; the

The Senior Partner

first indication re. the health of the office account. That aside, Nichols anyway seemed appalled at the ideas I had just propounded, perhaps because his earlier attempt to save his office account some cash was dashed by my impudent request. But forewarned as I was, I told him I would deal with the redecoration and with the acquisition of a PC and he could repay me over the coming months. I just felt that I would not feel comfortable accepting the *status-quo* on these two matters. Also, I wanted to make a go of the new job, and therefore wanted to make it clear that I would be happy to invest in my future. Whether that was a good or a bad thing to do did not really concern me at the time. Once Nichols and Pope had left, I told Denise and Sarah of my plans and they were both more than delighted. My hitherto rosy outlook of a future with the firm was now somewhat jaded but what had already taken place paled into insignificance compared with what was to come. In the meantime, I had worked on the conveyancing, comparing local lawyers' fees and settling on a fair rate for the work to do and had also managed to place some advertising with the local golf club. The office was tidied up and I brought in all my own legal texts to, if nothing else, make my office look like a lawyer's office. And the work came in.

Over the next few months Nichols was just an unwelcome nuisance. Nothing he ever engaged me with was to do with my work. It was just as though he wanted to be a nuisance but, as I said earlier, I really wanted to make a go of it. In fact his visits were so frequent that I wondered if he actually had any work to do. At one stage I even contemplated buying him out, but Elaine had her doubts. I concluded that, certainly with Nichols, I was not flavour of the month and was never likely to be but felt more like an unwelcome visitor. But [rather foolishly perhaps] I put it down to his concern about the business my office was to achieve to meet his business-plan targets. It transpired that he had no business plan, so his concern most probably centred round the office turnover just covering the costs of running the place. Another, later reason for his not being overly keen on me was because I wanted to re-arrange the office accounts. The procedure in place when I joined was to DX a payment request for whatever reason, for example a local authority search or the deposit on a client's purchase, or paying in cheques from clients, a procedure which from start to finish was often spread over three days in all, with cheques being DX'd back to the office, clearly a cumbersome way of managing a simple matter. This somewhat extended process meant that Denise could not refer to the cards to see whether the client had paid in any funds to cover disbursements of a sale / purchase transaction. Either this firm had not yet caught up with most other firms' accounting systems, or Nichols *et al* was trying to micro-manage the business much to the detriment of office efficiency; I believe it was a combination of both. To see the state of a client's account was frankly a bit of a bind having to requisition information from another office when all we really needed to do was pick up a card in a neighbouring room.

Ultimately I was authorised to make a two-hour plus car-journey to collect all the cards relating to my office, and at the same time as I was dealing with this, I suggested that we have a part-time bookkeeper from the accountant's office just down the road, to keep everything in good order, as I was not prepared to take on that bookkeeper / accounts' clerk role myself, nor should I have to. Nichols suggested that £2.00 per hour [!] would be a fair remuneration for the person we needed. Even then, that was a pittance. Another office account issue?

On reflection, I now believe that I had upset Nichols' cosy arrangement whereby he wanted things done as cheaply as possible and without having to deal with any little annoyances such as keeping his staff happy. However, two other matters arose. The first was that Nichols was calling the office and 'interrogating' Denise about what I was doing and had I sent out any bills. There were sometimes two or more calls a day. Denise didn't like it nor did I, and I asked her to refer the calls to me if I happened to be in the office when he called. Further, he had a rather bizarre approach to Sarah seemingly harbouring an intense dislike of her and suggesting, which was wholly inappropriate, that she was not operating as a family lawyer but running a social service, and that she was fat. [She was not 'fat']. I liken it now, knowing what transpired, to a kind of 'psyops' campaign to wear the poor girl down to the point where she would just go. Ultimately, he achieved what I, Sarah and Denise believed Nichols really wanted. Why he could not have just asked nicely for to leave and perhaps explain reasons for his decision, was [then] beyond me. As mooted above, I began to learn a lot about Nichols as I was later to be subjected to the same kind of pressure.

Things began to get even more odd. One day in March of 1989, after my being with the firm for approximately six months, Denise opened a newly delivered box of headed paper to discover that my name had been added as a partner. I had not received a call or a letter from the head office regarding my 'promotion'. There was absolutely no prior contact, no prior discussion, it just happened. It was obviously a decision made some days if not weeks before I found out, as the partners had time to have their headed paper re-printed to show my name. I was later informed [by Pope] that the firm's accounts had not been passed by the Law Society for the last financial year, 1987 / 88, [which means of course that and they were possibly in danger of being shut down]. It immediately occurred to me that this was the reason for my sudden elevation to salaried partner and I would not be at all surprised to learn that they had informed the Law Society that I was a partner long before I ever found out. Subsequently Nichols denied this. Bearing in mind that they engaged me in late September the previous year, did they then know that there would be issues with their accounts? The alternative was for the partnership to cease trading pending having the accounts signed off. They needed my practicing certificate to continue with their work. A legal executive, the previous incumbent, did not hold the necessary qualifications. I was further informed [by Pope] that an accounts assistant had been sacked and / or prosecuted because of 'accounts issues'.

Promotion to partner after six months or so? I did not sign any - or indeed even see - a partnership agreement. There are many things to consider about accepting a partnership, over twenty in all but at the time I was not then aware of them. It appears that Nichols was happy to put at risk my personal assets, including my family home, if the partnership became insolvent as a result of poor performance or a negligence claim that exceeded the professional indemnity insurance [PI] cover or was not able to cover its debts. On reflection, there was every reason to believe that the partnership was never a financially sound enterprise anyway. If there were insufficient funds in the partnership to cover liabilities, creditors could pursue individual partners in a traditional unlimited liability partnership [which the firm was] on a joint and several liability basis. That means a creditor could choose to pursue me rather than the other partners on the basis that I may have had a greater net worth than the other partners and even if the partnership agreement contained a mutual indemnity clause. In a way it explained Nichols' keen interest in my personal affairs and property interests. In any event it is not just a case of putting a name on the headed paper. At least Pope had the decency to ring me and tell me about the accounts issue, and, further, that Nichols was not the senior partner, but he and Nichols were equal partners.

One has to ask, was it done in case the partnership was insolvent, and he wanted my assets to be utilised to ease the burden on him? I doubt that I could have avoided liability just because I was not asked about becoming a partner, and then did nothing about him sticking my name on the firm's headed paper. I do not think that Nichols could have done that without the knowledge of Pope and Brooks. Another example of the firm's rather odd approach to partnership affairs? In my ignorance, I shrugged it off because I wanted to make a success of the office, and was working damn hard at it for very little money. Regarding my reimbursement for the decorating and PC costs, very little was happening even though the other two offices were asking Denise to upload their leases and do other work for them. On another issue, I asked if their head office could undertake applications [related to minor disputes basically] at the courts to save me spending probably three or four hours away from the office. The head office was a five minute walk. This was refused.

Had the partners asked me if I wanted to be a partner, I would have said no. I already believed the firm was not comfortable financially and there was no accommodating, friendly, outgoing and healthy relationship which I enjoyed in all other firms I worked with, and Nichols' approach to Sarah was frankly appalling. The cracks in the entire business were now obvious to me. My most severe criticism was that the business overall was just not viable, and that sooner or later the roof would fall in. There appeared to be no sound infrastructure at the office and I suspected that the other two offices were similarly disadvantaged. Pope and Brooks must have been aware of the reason for my rapid promotion, and that it was then a good way to overcome a very serious accounts issue. My suspicions were borne out by subsequent events.

*****

The Unravelling.

Denise, my very good secretary moved away with her husband who had been posted [he was in the military] and I got to work one Monday morning to find a new girl had been employed to take her place. I was unaware that Nichols was even interviewing for a replacement, nor was I asked to meet her at interview. Not exactly a crime but rather unusual. The new girl, Amanda, was not by any means a trained legal secretary, and barely managed the work, so it was, one can surmise, a 'cheap deal' for Nichols. I therefore asked my wife to pop in to help, which she willingly did a few days each week, and in return I paid the creche fees [from the office account] but no wages, so for Nichols it was a another 'cheap deal'. When Nichols turned up one day he met my wife, then told me in no uncertain terms that he did not agree to the arrangement. Pope later informed me that he once tried the same arrangement, and Nichols accused him of trying to 'take over' the office and that arrangement was also terminated. In any event, we managed to knock Amanda into shape, and she, the part-time bookkeeper and I managed to cope. I was now aware that Nichols and Pope had a love-hate relationship, but I never once considered that Pope was a person who did as he was told and just tagged along with whatever Nichols told him to do. However, and having tried to make contact with the guy [Pope – see the correspondence I sent to him – copied later in this report] I began to believe that he was fully aware of what Nichols was up to.

In June / July of 1991, our new house was nearing completion, so I wanted to sell my current home. I asked Nichols if he could deal with the sale as I could obviously not deal with it myself. He agreed, and another office [not the head-office] was instructed. I had been shedding my remaining business interests and the last house of my property portfolio and easily financed the new-build and it was fully costed. I had retained for interest purposes most of my old business information and I still have all my property purchase and sales particulars. The property sold quite quickly at £130,000, nearly twice what we had paid, and I left the net sale proceeds in my client account and withdrew funds as required to finish the build inter alia. What was paid out and to whom was clearly evidenced by entries on my card. I had by then sacked my builder for incompetence and was finishing the build myself, mainly plumbing, carpentry and decoration. After the sale we lived for about two weeks in a caravan on site until we moved in at mid- to-end of August of the same year. I now had two children.

There were still bizarre office episodes. Just after my sale some 'accountant' guy, apparently a friend of Nichols and not actually an accountant, turned up one day supposedly to do an audit. He hung around for a few days then told me that I should not have my own client account card in my office *'as it represented a breach of the accounts' rules'* I told him to take it away and keep it at the head office which in the light of no information to the contrary, I assume he did. At that time there was about £11,000 still on the card. Then Nichols would turn up at the office, sometimes dressed in motor-cycle leathers, and mooch about then plant himself in a chair just sitting looking at me, saying nothing. It was disconcerting to say the least, and on occasions I had to ask him if I could be of any assistance, or if he was feeling okay or needed to discuss anything with me. Ultimately, I would ask either the part-time bookkeeper or Amanda to ring me when the guy was in my office to remind me of a client appointment just to get rid of him. It appeared to be a successful ploy. He was also asking questions about my sale and new house, in particular how much land we owned. He very probably visited the place to 'sus it out' and if he did so I hope he was suitably impressed with the build. I now think this was more than a casual, incidental enquiry, engendered by his [as I now believe] interest in my personal affairs and what he was then plotting to get me removed from the office. It seemed my affairs were of interest and this notion is reinforced by what transpired only a few months later. It seems odd thinking about it now, but I also believe that the 'accountant's' visit and Nichols' odd behaviour seemed triggered my card being removed to the head office.

We had, like every law firm, good clients but a few bad ones, the ones who just - or appear to just - stay within the law regarding their business and personal affairs. I had one client turn up to deal with some of his buy-to-lets and once he outlined to me his plans, I suggested he would be better advised by his accountant who would no doubt be dealing with his self-assessment and other tax affairs. He said he didn't have an accountant, and collected his rents in cash and did not have any dealings with HMRC. The meeting lasted for about ten seconds more. I believe he had hoped that a small firm [like mine] would be happy to deal with him! My two worst were Stan, who ran a small manufacturing business, and a property developer, George whom I recall was thoroughly unpleasant to his wife on the occasions when they both visited the office. And he wanted everything done yesterday. Things came to a head one day when we were supposed to complete on a mortgage-funded purchase of business premises as a re-development deal but on the day of completion I discovered that the business was still occupied by the vendor and still hard at work. I have no idea whether this was some kind of 'deal' George had arranged with the vendor, and even after all the usual notices the vendor refused to leave and his own solicitor dumped him, so I had to send the funds back to the lender as they insisted [rightly] on vacant possession and would not accommodate any other option so I had to call the whole thing off. I told the client we had a cause of action suing for, inter alia, loss of bargain, but he seemed so wary about it, asking if I would deal with it 'personally' and not through the firm. He then wanted to find a business he could invest in, so I introduced him to Stan. George seemed pleased about the intro, but that too went horribly wrong. I had no financial interest in their businesses, nor did I want any. I had no sympathy for either of them as I believed they were more than a degree dishonest, manifested inter alia by their both being very reluctant to be open about their respective interests.

People in whom I had confided asked me why I didn't just leave the firm. I didn't need the money, and I was admittedly finding it all very stressful. It is a good point and on reflection I ask myself the same question. It now occurs to me that perhaps Nichols was also asking the same question, viz., 'Why does this guy put up with me? Why doesn't he leave?' But he took a more direct approach.

Shortly after my account card had been removed to Nichols' office, a number of incidents took place. The first was a 'phone call asking me whether I had paid the sum of £7,000 into their account. I assumed that meant the office account, as no payments into any specified client account would cause any concern and anyway payments to do with my clients' accounts would have been initiated from my office. There was no further information and I confess I had no idea what they were - then - talking about. It was Nichols again. It does seem odd; if such a transaction had taken place, why ask me? Suspicious as I have become about all these financial shenanigans, I now ask myself if Nichols himself transferred that sum to his office account from the £11,000 on my own card. Was it done to pay off an overdraft? Many possibilities arise, and nothing would surprise me now. But as far as I then knew, I still had around £11,000 credit on my card.

It must be made clear here that throughout my time at the firm my engagement with Pope was minimal, and with Fred Brooks there was none at all, and I have no idea of how those two worked with Nichols. Then perhaps oddest of all, Nichols turned up from time to time and seemed focussed on asking me how he could get rid of a partner. I felt like suggesting that was easy; just carry on as you are doing and I'll go, but instead I mentioned that he might just ask the partner concerned to leave. I did not wish to get involved in office politics, and in any event it was not an issue Nichols should be asking me. Were we back to the Sarah scenario, the poor women he drove away with a kind of psyops campaign. I now knew that Nichols had been a Service policeman, and to give him his due, he did pass the law exams so he cannot have been a total idiot, and no doubt he knew all about psyops, or more probably, it came naturally to him. But a few things began to fall into place and looking at it now and analysing the events, I came to believe that Nichols had, firstly, never wanted to employ another solicitor but had to due to the accounts problems and secondly that he really wanted to close the office I was running more so then as at that time there was only me, Amanda and the part-tine bookkeeper in the place. And to achieve that object he had to get rid of me, the guy he chose to [generously] appoint as a partner after only six months in office. If the foregoing was bad, things now took a very serious turn.

Was I immune to all these goings-on? No, I was not. Pressure was beginning to tell, in that before we saw out 1988/9 I began to suffer with migraines. I would try and nap during lunchtimes; I went straight to bed when I got home; I rarely slept properly, but spent most nights dozing fitfully, but never getting a good night's sleep; my weekends were a write-off. When at dawn I saw the light hitting the curtains, I knew I had to get out of bed and drive to work. It was an awful, long-lasting experience. My excellent doctor told me I was in the wrong job; he referred me to a specialist. I took Imigran and Amitriptyline but they seemed to help very little.

Being in the law is in any event stressful. A report by Staci Zaretsky, quoting American Bar Association Commission on Lawyer Assistance Programme, she noted;

> *'Members of the legal profession struggle with mental-health and wellness issues thanks to the near-constant stress that they face on a daily basis. Twenty-one percent of licensed, employed attorneys qualify as problem drinkers, 28 percent struggle with some level of depression, and 19 percent demonstrate symptoms of anxiety'.*

Does this apply equally to the UK? Yes. To quote LawCare, a non-profit organization offering mental health, legal counselling, and rehabilitation services;

> *'More than 50 per cent of the profession felt stressed and that 19 per cent were suffering from clinical depression. That is one fifth of the profession suffering from mostly avoidable and preventable mental ill health. Employers can*

also do more to help people who manage long-term mental health conditions, which are perfectly manageable and do not cause increased absence from work. Now and then I do hear encouraging stories of employers doing the right thing in this arena. But they are still too few and far between'.

In 2013, the Law Society interviewed 2,226 solicitors about stress at work and, shockingly, more than 95 per cent said their stress was extreme or severe; in 2014, 36 per cent of 'stressed-out' calls to LawCare were from solicitors below five years PQE, indicating that the future of the profession is already stressed before reaching the higher echelons. That is not much of a succession plan. It is fortunate for those now in the profession that the stress is recognised, and action can be taken to reduce it, but at the time I am talking about it was a case of being told to 'Man Up' and get with it. However, the causes and effects were still the same then as they are now.

It was also at about this time that Nichols took on a clerk, David S, who appeared in my office one day to say that Nichols had sent him to work with me for a while; he had no special brief, nor had I any idea what he was supposed to be doing, so I gave him a few will-drafting jobs, then after a few days he - rather shamefacedly - confessed to me that Nichols had sent him to the office to spy on me! Spooky or what? The lad is probably, and hopefully, working somewhere as a solicitor as he seemed a decent guy. Then came another piece of delightful news, call to say that the client account was overdrawn so of course I assumed he was telling me because it was something to do with my clients' accounts. I still did not then know whether the three offices just held all their clients' money on one account or in three separate accounts, viz., one for each office [which would have been the sensible option] so if it had been my account, then the next thing would quite naturally have been for Nichols or maybe his 'accountant' to visit the office and trawl through the accounts. However, I heard nothing more which was both a relief and also odd that I as a partner, was not told that it was [possibly, I never found out] a mistake and all was well. To have a client account overdrawn is probably the closest disaster to arriving home and finding your house burnt down. Was this another move on Nichols' chessboard? Was he also feeding this stuff to his other two partners, to prepare them ready for the 'Big Accusation'?

Then one evening, as I was leaving the office, Pope turned up as I was locking the front door. He asked if we could have a word, so I sat in his car with him and he asked me if I was holding onto or 'controlling' monies. I had no idea what he was talking about, and I got the impression that he had no idea either, but had either been sent by Nichols or had perhaps been told by him that there might be an issue of 'missing money' but what practically appeared to me to be an accusation of theft, was just too much to accept. Pope was unable to expand on the scenario he was apparently addressing, and I thought he might have been sent possibly as an attempt to reel him into some little conspiracy which I [now] know Nichols had been working on in an effort to oust me - and worse. Pope was unable to be specific and I concluded that he might have heard something from his 'senior partner' Nichols re. the accounts and which so disturbed the guy [who then seemed a decent fellow] that he took on a solo mission. After the meeting, brief though it was, I decided I'd had enough.

Another little point arises. If any person in a business is suspected of wrongdoing, it would be normal to confront the individual concerned and lay out the case in as much detail as possible and then seek a response. Although there was a 'meeting' of sorts, see infra, it was by then too late and secondly it was clearly not one which was meant to be a sensible discussion to address the issue, rather one engineered as an opportunity for Nichols to be insulting and not sensibly discuss the issues as he saw them. However, no such 'pre-action' meeting took place and, had it, I could then have asked to see my card account as it was the only medium I ever used for my own payments which were possibly catalogued by Nichols to make up the *schedule of payments* apparently produced at the trial [which in fact I never saw; it was mentioned by the CCRC]. If indeed there were genuine concerns about my account, it would have taken minutes to deal with. I have to conclude that Nichols did not want the issues 'cleared up' firstly because there were none, and secondly he had some other course of action in mind. Being a former Service acting corporal policeman, the man would know all about the proper processes, and doubtless he had carried out many interviews with 'suspects' and for whom I have the utmost sympathy.

However, the Pope meeting was the last straw. I'd had enough, so the next morning I called Nichols and told him I was leaving. I regarded it as constructive dismissal. A locum [Charles] who had worked there from time to time came into the office and I handed over to him. In the few days it took to do the handover, my agent found me a locum position - and I told Charles the small town where I was going to work - and I commenced working there almost immediately. My agent told me later that he had a call from Nichols but he said the description he used of me was so alarming and denigrating that he ignored it. The guy Nichols described was not the guy my agent had used so successfully for many assignments in the past.

Then I got a call from Nichols asking if I would pop into my old office for a chat. I agreed to do this, and on meeting him, Pope and David [the clerk] were also there. I thought that David's presence was a bit inappropriate, but nevertheless, I sat down and prepared for some meaningful dialogue. However, Nichols opening words to me were, '*I never knew we had a tealeaf in the firm*'. I then knew this was not going to be, or was never intended to be, a sensible discussion of 'events'. Then he told me that he had spoken to my old builder, the one I sacked, who told him that I had agreed to do all future work for him at a reduced rate. No I had not, and in any event I had not acted for the guy and when I left the firm I had no files open for him and had no intention of doing any work for him. I told Nichols that he was being naïve to believe that, and seeing there was no point in staying as clearly we were not going to resolve the issues he seemed concerned about, I just left. It took Nichols less than a week to locate my new employer to inform him [I assume] that I had been making off with clients' money; clearly my new boss had no option but to 'let me go'.

On the same day, sometime in October / November 1991 I believe, my wife called to say that two police officers had called at the house asking for me, and would I drop into the police station on the way home. This I did. The real nightmare had begun. The cops told me that Nichols had laid a complaint that I had stolen money from the clients' account. I denied it. I could just not identify with what they were saying. Their line of questioning was, basically, *'What did you do with the money?'* It seems a very odd thing to ask, as, whenever money from either office or clients' accounts is moved it is always evidenced by a requisition slip and then a cheque; cash is never taken out of a client's account, and from the office account usually only for petty cash uses. They referred to no documents, made no specific allegations because, frankly, they could not; there had been no 'thefts' or certainly not by me.

A few days later I received in the post a county court summons; it was from Nichols claiming the sum of £3,500 or thereabouts, and oddly [for a solicitor that is] he had added at the end of his statement of claim *'I know he can afford it'* as though this might make it more difficult to defend, or because Nichols just had no idea about how to draft a statement of claim. That remark is [probably] indicative of the fact that he had seen my client card and knew what had been paid in on the sale of my house in 1991 and must have known that I still had a balance of £11,000 in credit [unless he had removed the odd £7,000 – see supra]. I never had any idea what Nichols actually did in his business, but it certainly was not drafting statements of claim. I entered a defence and heard no more. However, mindful of the fact that I still had that money on my account with his firm, and as I never saw my card again, it is perfectly possible that Nichols just took the money from my account. I often thought that I should just go to the bank [Barclays] and get it back, but I knew I couldn't, firstly, and secondly, I did not want to give Nichols the satisfaction of denying my request if I were to ask him for it, and anyway I believed there would be a better opportunity of recovering it when this very odd business was sorted out eventually. In the event, I just overlooked it, not surprisingly because the situation became very serious and contentious.

You will note [later] that appeals were more on procedural and capacity issues than evidential, and I tend to believe that counsel's opinion on taking up this case was that the prosecution had the case 'sewn up'; hence, perhaps, the pressure on me via the clerk to enter a guilty plea, of which see later. I was now unemployed, probably unemployable and suffering severe long-lasting migraines. Migraine is a neurological condition that can cause multiple symptoms. It's frequently characterized by intense, debilitating headaches. Symptoms may include nausea, vomiting, difficulty speaking, numbness or tingling, and sensitivity to light and sound. Migraines often run in families and affect all ages. Not fun at all.

*****

My Tormentor.

Having had to engage with the main accuser for three years, and what he had done to me and others over that period I feel qualified to comment on his behaviour. I believe he is a sociopath. He is certainly a bully. A sociopath uses 'mind games' to control people and shows a lack of regard for others' feelings or for violations of people's rights and does not respect social norms or laws. They also, inter alia, lie, deceive others, use others for personal gain and feel no remorse for having mistreated people. In addition, they do not show emotions, they have a sense of superiority and strong, unwavering opinions; unable to keep positive friendships and relationships. Symptoms include breaking rules without regard for the consequences. There are other symptoms and not all of the above may apply. However, I think I have set out enough for one to understand that, if what I am suggesting is true, then I have a correct diagnosis. Abuse at work generally is one thing, but to be targeted by an abuser and bully over long periods is quite another.

I engaged a firm of solicitors to deal with the allegations, and had a first meeting with a barrister whose chambers were over an hour's drive from the solicitor's office. Why there I don't understand, as the nearest chambers were only a thirty minute drive away, but I really cannot recall what took place at that meeting as I spent most of my time sitting in reception. When I did see the barrister, he looked to me a bit like a ladies' hairdresser, and vain with it. I estimate that I saw the lawyers no more than four times in all between then and trial. I was eventually charged with theft, and naturally had to appear in the local magistrates' court. The initial charge was that I had stolen the sum of £3,500.00. We've seen that figure before. It seems odd that Nichols had earlier tried to recover that sum from me as a debt owed when he actually believed I had stolen it. Eventually, I was remanded to the crown court for trial. Somewhat oddly, my ex-builder turned up whenever I had to appear in the magistrates' court, and I doubt he was an ardent scrutineer of the court listings; who alerted him? I wonder. After one of those hearings, he followed me into the street and yelled out, 'Bent solicitor!' And on another occasion I came across him at a petrol station and I was again subjected to abuse. Nice man.

I must now make a number of points; firstly, as I had been charged within months of my leaving the firm, all the documents relating to my clients' transactions, viz., all the files, conveyancing completion statements, bank statements, office payments, clients' funds in and out and cheque requisition slips and cheques and even my own client account card would all be available, and in addition, all the prosecution statements would be readily available for me and my defence team to see. However, between charge and trial date I did not see any of the above documents. Nor do I know what my lawyers were working on. And the period between charge and trial was three and a half years. Forty-two months. In addition, I recall that on the day the trial started, the prosecution had to amend the offences with which I was charged. We are not here talking about Covid 19 or any pandemic time. We are talking about between August 1991 January 1995 when the waiting time to get to court was measured in months not years. The trial took place over three weeks, and of that I remember only the first two days or so, and am not surprised as temporary memory loss can be brought on by stress, depression, anxiety, prescription medication, fatigue and sleep deprivation; all of those ailments affected me being in this awfully serious situation. Thereafter I remembered very little. The points I remember clearly are:-

1. When discussing capacity, and my migraines, the prosecuting barrister said that he gets migraines and it didn't stop him from

working; he should have been addressed on that. There are migraines and there are migraines.

2. Nichols saying at one point that he and I were friends; we were never friends.

3. Nichols for some reason bringing up the fact of my wife working in the office; I failed to see the relevance of that unless he was suggesting some conspiracy with her to steal clients' money - but he added afterwards that 'she was scruffy'.

4. My builder saying that he was surprised to have been paid with a client account cheque. [see supra]. At the time that did not register with me but it has now taken on some significance as I had my own client funds, but bearing in mind what transpired it was a very telling remark. If my defence team had applied to the prosecution to produce my client account card, which they had not, or if they had applied it was not produced, it would have shown the payments to the builder as well as all the other payments which no doubt appeared on the 'auditors schedule' [see below] and shown to the jury. It would have been game over for the prosecution.

In my eventual communications with the CCRC a good few years later, they mention this 'schedule of offences' [about which I knew nothing at the time] presented by an auditor called by the prosecution, and later that *'there was no dispute that the defendant had carried out the transactions alleged'* this is absolute nonsense as I never saw the schedule, but if it represented an unadulterated copy of my own client account card, then indeed I could have agreed it, but I do not recall any agreed facts between prosecution

The Senior Partner

and defence, *'and that he has used client accounts'* - [no, I used my own account] – *'in order to pay his builder [who was building a house for him] after making payments into them'** [I don't understand what is being said here] and - *'he accepted that he had stretched the accounts rules ... but denied that he had ever acted dishonestly'*. Possibly correct from what Nichols' 'accountant' told me. On this, refer to the 'accountant's' visit when he removed my client account card from my office, with a balance of £11,000.

*NB – and this is important; the only payment into my account which was opened simply and only for my sale transaction, was the proceeds of my house sale, being £130,000 less disbursements. *There were no other 'payments'* as stated above, and this would be borne out by my client account card which Nichols had in his constructive possession over the whole period of this business, and which would clearly show that all and any payments out were made from my own funds. I have no doubt that the 'schedule' above was made up of payments I had quite legitimately made from my own funds. However, this an assumption as I never saw the 'schedule'.

Back to the builder and the client account cheque; when my builder stood up and said that *'he was surprised to have had his account paid by a client account cheque'* he was talking in 1995 about a cheque or cheques he had received from me four years after he received the cheque / cheques. Three points arise here; firstly, Nichols could only have had that information from my client card so he must have used other information from it to arrive at the total allegedly 'stolen'; secondly, Nichols would have seen the total expenditure from my card as approximately £90k; thirdly unless the builder had been 'coached' I seriously doubt whether he knew the difference between a client account cheque and an office account cheque, and who anyway probably didn't care either way. And bearing in mind the reference to my builder at the abortive meeting mentioned above, and that I had sacked the man, I am led to the inevitable conclusion that Nichols and my former builder had entered into some unholy alliance to bring about a conviction, or at the very least support the prosecution case. My barrister, as far as I recall, did not question the builder on this point.

Another issue: my case was being managed by a solicitors' clerk and with all due respect for the guy, I don't believe he should have had conduct of my case, and incidentally, was constantly telling me that I should plead guilty to the charges, but I refused to agree to do so. Consider; why was he was asking? Was it because he took it upon himself to push the point? I doubt it. More realistically counsel had asked him to suggest a guilty plea; did counsel think he was trying to defend the indefensible? If counsel actually had sight of my client account card and all the documents available in 1991, it would have presented a whole new picture and he would not try to push me into a guilty plea? I doubt it. Had the 'schedule of payments' apparently presented by the auditor actually been drafted using the entries on my own card or made up by Nichols to show a series of 'extractions' from possibly hundreds of clients' cards which apparently over a period of just over two years [July 1989 to say, August 1991] in total to a sum of £90,000 to present a situation other than the facts suggested? If the card as removed from my office had been part of the auditors instructions, and had been prepared on that basis, then quite simply there would be no case to answer.

Game Over?

At the end of the prosecution case, I just told my barrister that I could not give evidence in my defence, the reasons were manifold. At the material time I was unable to even think straight, but I had some fixation that it was something to do with a breach of the accounts rules. [The 'accountant' again]. I sometimes wonder how it was that I could be so affected by stress that I could not function normally. I know now that the effects of stress are insidious; they creep up on one and I had at the time of trial been under severe stress for a period of four and a half years, and in addition, the migraine. There had been a start date some six months previously, but that was abandoned after half a day as Nichols had approached members of the jury during the lunchbreak.

It might be relevant here to discuss the trial process particularly in view of the criticisms I have of the defence. Ours is an adversarial system, whereby the judge just listens to the defence and prosecution barristers setting out their cases on the evidence they have been given by their solicitors. The judge does not normally interfere with their delivery nor challenge any of the evidence. It is essentially the same system as used in America, probably the worst of the civilised countries in the world for miscarriages of justice. Their and our system is based around the idea that you can get to the truth when two opposing sides make their cases in court. But what happens if your barrister is so overloaded he can't handle the case that could cost you your freedom? What if the prosecution barrister totally outclasses the defence barrister in experience, delivery and grasp of the essentials so leaving the opposition standing? What happens when the most important testimony goes unheard, or when the evidence that could prove your innocence goes unseen? These failures aren't hypothetical. They happen all the time. How would the other form of hearing be different? The inquisitorial system is where the judge takes an active role, looking for evidence, questioning witnesses and getting involved in the process as he deems fit. Many EU countries use this system, including France and Italy. However, Andrew Perkins of Ashford's, solicitors, reinforcing the above issues, says that there is a perceived unfairness in the adversarial legal system in situations where the parties do not have 'equality of arms'; a better resourced party may be more able to gather evidence and present a stronger case to the Judge than their opposition. Furthermore, because the parties have near complete conduct of the case from start to judgment, they are able to choose what evidence they put before the Court. How true in my case.

By comparison, in an inquisitorial system the Judge is involved throughout the process and actually steers the collation and preparation of evidence. He is therefore able to decide what evidence is admitted by both parties, before questioning the witnesses himself and going on to make an informed decision on the outcome. Perkins adds that even though an English Judge may not decide what matters to investigate and how to do so, his role is by no means passive. Under the Civil Procedure Rules which came into force in 1999 [four years after my case], the Court has very wide case-management powers which are used to ensure that the dispute is resolved efficiently and in accordance with the CPR's overriding objective of enabling the Court to deal with cases justly and at a proportionate cost. The Court will do so by excluding superfluous evidence, managing the parties' costs, and setting a strict timetable to trial under threat of sanction should any of the dates be missed. It may well be the case that these rules been in force in 1995, my judge may well have become involved as, to run such a case as mine over fifteen working days, was a trial for all parties concerned.

As it was, I had no idea what it was I had done wrong, I could not organise my thoughts, and as I said, of the prosecution case I remember only the first few days. On reflection, had I even seen the 'schedule' referred to above, I might well have had a fighting chance of saying something positive. When I told my barrister I would not give evidence, he responded by saying that it was probably for the best *'as the prosecution would tear you to pieces'*. Or words to that effect; perhaps his comment was a bit unprofessional and I wonder still whether counsel was relieved for his own reasons, i.e., did he have another brief on the way or did he just think that the weight of evidence against me was overwhelmingly in favour of the prosecution? Or was he concerned that the legal aid fund was not paying him enough? With the benefit of hindsight, I believe that counsel should have applied for a delay in the presentation of the defence submission, not just told the judge that I would not be submitting evidence in my defence. It might then have been possible for all concerned to go over the prosecution evidence to at least give me a chance. Unfortunately, I do not think that was an option then. This gave the jury no option but to convict. [See comment later]. Only counsel can explain his actions. The inevitable result of my abandoning my right to give evidence was a conviction.

The Senior Partner

When the judge heard the guilty verdict, he addressed me saying that I *'would not be going home tonight'*. I was taken down to the court cells, later handcuffed and put into a prison van with a number of other detainees and taken to the local prison to be held on remand pending sentencing. I was numb. On arrival at prison, I was finger-printed and photographed, given prison clothes to wear and then taken to a single cell as I was supposed to be on self-harm watch. After a few days, I was taken to the main block to share a cell with one other person. I had become an object. I had joined the other eighty to ninety thousand people who had fallen to the bottom rung of the social ladder, people who for the rest of their lives will have to live with the fact that they have been to jail, and in many cases will never be able to return to a normal life. It makes no difference whether it was for a week or ten years; the scars are the same and why? Some deserved it; many did not.

Once I had become used to the routine, I had time to think, to analyse. Prison is not a punishment except [in my case anyway] to the mind. It is how one regards oneself being in that position. To me I feel that my history has been wiped out, that I am no longer the person I was, and even more so because I know I have not committed any crime, but the main priority for me was to serve my time. I knew I would have to appeal. As I saw it then, there were two main arguments to pursue; firstly, that I was not fit to stand trial, as my doctor and my neurologist had surmised and that for anybody to have to wait for three and a half years for trial is grossly unfair. What is the effect on those persons? It very much depends on the individual. And did at any time my lawyers apply to the court [CPS] to establish the cause of the delay? Not to my knowledge. Dwelling for too long on one's own problems about which I could then do nothing, was not going to do me any good. I turned my attention to the system which now held me in custody.

At great expense to the public purse, I was being clothed, fed and kept comfortably warm. I did not have to earn my keep and I was also paid an allowance for the purchase of essentials such as soap and toothpaste. Others use their money to buy cigarettes and 'phone cards. Both were a form of currency in jail, these days of course the main currency is drugs. It also occurred to me that, and as my writer [Edd] says in his book on the criminal justice system, there are many people in jail who should not be there, viz., the ones who would never again engage with the criminal justice system, and those who are innocent but convicted. Bearing in mind that every year there are about a thousand successful appeals against conviction in the UK, and doubtless many more applications which were refused. One ought therefore turn to the procedures of which more later. For the others who should be in jail, prison is just a temporary inconvenience, and as we know the recidivism rate is well over fifty percent, so prison is clearly not a deterrent. My cell-mate was Richard, sent down for eighteen months for [what he said] was a minor drug offence. He actually seemed a decent bloke, but he was from Canada. His incarceration was costing the taxpayer about £40,000. Why was he not just sent back home and marked as being *persona-non-grata* and not allowed back to the UK? Again from the same book. 'Judges put petty criminals in prison 'out of ignorance".

I know Edd spent a lot of his legal career dealing with criminal work, and I agreed wholeheartedly with comments he made about this case. When he was doing his education degree, he taught adults with severe learning difficulties and prison inmates; they both needed education and engagement with different peer groups as much as each other. Punishment was not, he concluded, the way to deal with most criminals and he has long been an exponent of the idea that prison does not work, so why were there so many people in jail? Sentences of less than two years or thereabouts are pointless. In cases involving violence, where there is a clear need to protect the public, then short sentences are obviously no deterrent and therefore pointless because over such a short period the prison service cannot carry out the aims it was established to do, viz; *'to help those sentenced to custody to lead law-abiding and useful lives.'* There can be no effective [or any] rehabilitation; there can be no worthwhile education programme as there is [anyway] a shortage of education staff and the prisons' education budget is far too small; there is almost uncontrolled violence and drug-abuse in prison; there is a shortage of prison officers. All a short sentence does is remove the fear of prison as a deterrent, so is totally counter-productive.

I looked at the Civitas report *'Who Goes To Prison'*. Recidivism costs the UK £13 billion pa. [2016 figure]; seventy percent of prison sentences are imposed on criminals with at least seven previous convictions. And fifty percent are imposed on offenders with fifteen or more recorded crimes. Fewer than one in twelve prisoners is inside for a first offence, about 7,000 people currently, and where they are in jail, it is usually for a crime *of extreme violence* or *sex offences*. That is encouraging but raises two points. One; offences of violence do not warrant a short sentence and two, who, then, would be serving short sentences? It seems that for extreme violence / sex offences, a longer term is reasonable, and it is pointless to jail a person for e.g., a serious speeding offence, or a person unlikely to re-offend [such as Jonathan Aitkin or Lord Archer, or maybe lawyers and other professionals] and who rarely pose a danger to the public. Nobody should go to jail for a first offence [except where there is a danger to the public, obviously] so other sanctions should be imposed where a period of probation or community service may well have a deterrent effect, and overall do more good, and be substantially cheaper than a spell in jail. There might be a case for all sentences of a year or less being wiped from the offenders' record to give all those so effected a fair 'second chance' in life. Indeed, they could even in extreme cases have recourse to law for compensation on the basis that the prison service had failed them. It is also difficult to understand how jailing me would *'help me to lead law-abiding and useful life ...'* when instead it would, or could, as with similar cases and defendants, destroy family life, make us unemployable, forever bear a grudge against the criminal justice system thereby having a totally negative effect on us for the rest of our lives which could otherwise be spent in the serving the public.

Consider also extended sentences, [Letter, Peter Dawson, Director, Prison Reform Trust. Times 7 October 2020].

> *"People now go to prison for much longer than they used to for the same crimes. The average prison sentence is more than two years longer now than it was in 2007. Prison*

conditions have also deteriorated over the past decade. As our report published this week drawing evidence from 85 prisons says for anyone whose release depends on parole there is also the possibility that lack of opportunity to progress will end up delaying when they cannot get out sometimes for a matter of years. Court of Appeal guidance is a modest recognition that the impact of going to prison ... is now more severe than the law assumes. The government should plan to end overcrowding and make prisons the decent, rehabilitative environment that the public has a right to expect."

Fighting Back.

After my release, my barrister appealed in June 1995 to a single judge on the basis of a number of issues relating principally to capacity and the judge's directions during trial; appeal refused. A further appeal was made to a full court in July 1995 on roughly the same grounds was again refused. I do not know whether because of my then professional status they raised the bar, or refused on other grounds.

In any event, in June 2020 I got in contact with the CCRC. The points I raised [edited for length and with some additions] were as follows:

'I want you to look at the conviction. I did not give evidence in my defence. The first thing you will note about this case it that it is 25 years old. However, I believe there are issues which can be addressed by some of the characters who were involved, namely, the former partners of the firm Nichols, Pope. Certainly Pope can, after all this time, be utterly candid about his partner, Nichols and his goings-on as can the solicitors who acted for me, dealt with by their clerk, and counsel, and possibly the Law Society who [no doubt] were involved at some stage. However, I sincerely believe there are sufficient grounds for this to be referred to the Court of Appeal. Any person with even a modicum of legal knowledge can see that there are certain issues which do not add up. I trust you will agree. The prosecution case is that *'Between 1989 and 1991 I got myself into financial difficulties, and it is alleged that in order to alleviate my financial difficulties I transferred money from the accounts of my employers and clients to my own account or for my own use to pay private debts. It was alleged that I did so dishonestly without the authority of my employer or clients. The total sum involved was alleged to be some £90,000.'*

I will examine these allegations later in this missive. Nichols, as the prime mover in the prosecution had most definitely manipulated evidence to make it seem as though I had stolen funds from the clients' accounts and his office account. Further, the question of my being unfit to take the stand was valid; the prosecution delay in bringing the matter to court - it took three and a half years and for no apparent reason - had a serious and adverse effect on my capacity. I believe all the points listed in this book are worthy of consideration. I have lived with this for, at the date hereof, for almost 30 years; every day this business entered my head. I think it is time the whole matter is re-addressed. I am fed up with hiding behind aliases and nom-de-plumes; I cannot take my kids to America; or visit family in NZ or Australia; I cannot work in the law; I am always fearful of hearing once again, *'... what have you been up to ...?* I have had to face the task of re-inventing myself, carving out new careers. For reasons I will go into here I have come to realise after all this time that the whole business of my prosecution was badly overseen by the CPS and by my defence; obvious points on both sides were ignored, and particularly because the prosecution had a duty to disclose evidence which may be helpful to the defence. There has been a gross miscarriage of justice. You will note the extraordinary series of events, and that neither I nor my legal team had sight of the documents [very possibly because they did not bother to even consider applying for them if indeed they knew anything at all about solicitors' accounts] one would expect to see on a case such as this, for example, copies of cheques, client account cards, requisition / transaction slips. This is odd, as there is no way any of the alleged offences could have taken place without leaving a paper trail, and not the artificial one concocted by Nichols.

Many aspects of the whole business are just surreal; the behaviour of just one man; the events during my time with the firm; the capacity aspect; the lack of evidence; the prosecution took three weeks to present their case and with the average trial length being three to five days this is just extraordinary. Then the judge's post-sentencing admonishment of counsel. I thought the sentence was a little harsh bearing in mind the generally poor state of the firm I was then working for and in particular their appalling accounts record. As an aside, one has to ask, did the chaotic state of the firm's accounts provide a means for the accuser to fabricate evidence? To lay at my door any serious issues dogging their accounts? These are rhetorical questions of course, but they do still colour the whole business just the same.

I repeat, at no time was I ever invited to go through the accounts with the partners to establish the issues which so concerned them so they could be dealt with. The last thing any firm wants is to have itself dragged through the courts, but to my mind the one person who was behind all this was Nichols. He wanted a prosecution. I may be wrong, but I am sure this was not the wishes of the other partners. You will note that at least one of them, Pope, had the opportunity to take Nichols to task, but failed to do so.

Further approach to the CCRC

1. My barrister applied to you in 1995 on the ground that I was unfit for trial, and certainly unfit to go through the defence case. The prosecution took three weeks to present their case which was an extraordinary period of time and as mentioned later, 90% of it went over my head and it is reasonable to suppose that the jury must have felt the same. Murder trials are sometimes dealt with well within such periods. I suspect the judge was also getting fed up with it. You [CCRC] rejected my application as you stated that '*The* [solicitor's] *clerk, said you were acting normally*'. Or words to that effect. In truth, the clerk had only known me for the three weeks of the trial. He did not *know me* at all and certainly not in any 'normal' settings or circumstances. Further, at my sentencing the judge spent a good half hour [at least] laying into my defence barrister. I do not think he was being complimentary. Doubtless counsel will remember it. Two other issues come to mind.

2. A man turned up at my house [my wife was also there] before trial as he had 'heard' that I had 'substantial funds' stashed away in overseas accounts ... it was so ridiculous as to be laughable. I

might suggest that this was another Nichols ploy floated for some crazy notion of his, one might surmise, because he was unable to show definitely the destination of any funds he wanted to add to the toll as being 'stolen by me'. I never knew who the visitor was and never heard from him again. [Addition: *I was then so 'out of it' that I didn't even ask for his name of to see any ID. In fact, the whole idea of somebody turning up out of the blue and asking this was ridiculous; did he think I would confess if I had one? And from whom did that 'information' come? What was he expecting me to say?*

3. Some of the evidence at the start of the trail related to my capacity. On conviction the judge put me on self-harm register; if the judge thought I was of such unbalanced mind as to be suicidal, then surely I was not fit to proceed with the defence. At the end of the prosecution case, I told counsel that I could not go through with it; I was not fit. He added that '*The prosecution would tear you to shreds*' or words to that effect. I hardly think that was an appropriate remark to make. However, at that time Counsel was not playing with a full deck of cards. Further, I am positive that everybody concerned with the trial was more than a little fed up with it.

4. The case is as set out above. At the time of my conviction I had no idea of the charges of which I was found guilty. As a matter of fact, even though no evidence was given in my defence, the verdict was not unanimous.

5. Re capacity. I was on amitriptyline and other medication during the case, and before, for Migraines suffered during my time

with the firm [which went out of business after my trial] and so severe as to be totally debilitating; add lack of sleep and that they went on for many days or sometimes for a week or more and I am positive that my endeavours to make the new job work well, added to the odd behaviour of Nichols just meant that with stress-levels off the scale I was really doing myself no good at all. My own doctor told me the solution was to get another job. Amitriptyline side effects include impairment of thinking or reactions; be careful if you drive or do anything that requires you to be alert; confusion; difficulty in speaking; disturbed concentration; fear or nervousness; general feeling of tiredness or weakness.

6. After I joined the firm in 1988, I became very busy, and was producing a good turnover. [The problems with accounts, office decoration and purchase of a PC are all aired above].

7. At the same time I was already in the process of building my new house on land I purchased in December 1987 or thereabouts when I sold my other houses and I also had invested in that property the sale proceeds of my businesses. We were not hard up.

Other issues I set out have already been addressed, so I will move on to a summary of issues and some relating to accounts.

Summary:

1. Nichols was disingenuous re. my appointment to partner.

2. His behaviour during my employment with the firm was bizarre.

3. The issues raised by my ex-builder were easily refuted and I suspect 'tutoring' by Nichols.

4. Saw NO cheques evidencing payments made to me or any person or business related to me.

5. Saw NO client account cards; so no idea which clients had allegedly 'lost' money.

6. Saw NO transaction slips.

7. Prosecution did not ask to see my or my wife's bank statements.

8. Was shown NO evidence that any clients suffered any loss.

9. Why did I see no prosecution witness statements.

Were my lawyers incompetent?

10. Why did the prosecution take three weeks to present its case.

11. What is the protocol re. fraud charges and juries today.

12. Who – if there was one – was the auditor involved in the case.

13. Why did the judge put me on 'self-harm' watch'.

14. I have a sneaking suspicion that Nichols invented the alleged loss to the clients.

15. Re the firm's accounts.

   - We have a firm whose accounts were at one stage [at least] not passed by the Law society at a time when I was not involved with the firm.
   - Nichols asking me to understate my salary.
   - The credit of £7,000 [see 10 above] which he thought was from me; bad record keeping? Another Nichols invention?
   - Suggesting he could employ people for £2. per hour.
   - The firms bad payment record with the stationery supplier.
   - A certain accounts clerk being dismissed [or otherwise removed].
   - Sarah being 'pushed out'; was it a wage payment issue?

The claim Nichols issued against me personally and which was discontinued. On this, I received no 'letter before action' as the protocol demands, but now I think two issues arise; was he trying to recover from me the office decorating, PC purchase and other repayments I had claimed? Or did he see from payments made by me from my own client account card an opportunity to take matters to the extent that he did?

Consider also; the firms accounts were passed, I assume, periods 1988/89, 1989/90 and 1990/91 which seem to cover my period with the firm, so how can Nichols allege that I had been extracting funds over that period without it coming to light sometime in 1989 which he alleged was when the 'stealing' commenced?

The alleged theft was a sum of £90,000, a staggering amount of money [£100 pounds in 1991 is equivalent to £205.19 pounds in 2022] over a period of two years means £3,750 per month. Sums such as this would come to light immediately, not years after I joined the firm, I could not have taken it from my clients, as [see above] my business was conveyancing, and all my cases completed on time, and were all recorded on the appropriate client account card. In 1991, the firm still had all their client accounts on the old card system, so it would have been easy for any accountant forensic or otherwise, to see at the time of the alleged theft, that I had just sold my property for around £130,000, could there have been a suggestion that I started taking money before that? If that were the case, then it would have come to light then and there. Or did Nichols not disclose their existence?

So what happened? I believe Nichols had issues. I do not think he wanted to engage me; he looked upon me as a person who knew his own mind and just got on with his job and he may have felt that I was a threat of some kind, but maybe needed me initially to get them past the Law Society account problem, and from then on I was expendable ['NB; 'How do I get rid of a partner']. I'm sure my predecessor couldn't wait to leave. Why not? I do not know. Maybe one of the other partners does know. If Nichols had issues with my clients he certainly did not ask me about them. He knew that as regards any other issues, there was no paper trail to show I had taken any money as he suggested, so he must have had some difficulty convincing the CPS that was the case; he manufactured a case by no doubt using the payments I made from my legitimately held funds for the purposes shown on the cheques.

One has to ask, when did the accountants take control of the case? Did any ever get involved? Or did Nichols himself become the 'accountant' and file a list of transactions including the payment/s to my former builder? Did he attach my client account card? Did he tell the persons involved that I had sold my property in 1991? I very much doubt it. Was evidence withheld? Yes, it most certainly was. Did the builder and George the developer want to see me prosecuted? Yes. I've mentioned the builder; the developer's business failed [look at the Companies House info] and so did his involvement with the Stan, and did he blame me? I have no doubt. Was George an honest person? Most definitely he was not. Knowing Nichols it is easy to imagine him getting my builder to say whatever he wanted him to say.

I have come to believe that Nichols did not want to engage me or anybody else; from day one his attitude towards me made that obvious. I stuck with it because I wanted to make a go of it. Did Nichols make a claim on the Law Society's PI policy? It is worth looking at this as, whatever answer Nichols would give, he will be between a rock and a hard place.

I suggest that the firm was dysfunctional; they had staffing and financial issues, and I do not doubt that the other partners were having a hard time dealing with those matters and the behaviour of Nichols, and I would also suggest that virtually from the very beginning of my engagement with them that there was a real power struggle going on as to whether my office should be closed or remain open once the accounts issue with the Law Society was settled. I was piggy-in-the middle. I am also convinced that Nichols wanted it closed and more seriously, that he took the opportunity to heap onto my shoulders all the financial and other ills which dogged his business, when in fact, in my view anyway, it was poorly managed and there was bad blood between him and the other partners who seemed to me to be decent people.

No-go this time.

The CCRC decided not to take up the case. They by the way are to be congratulated on securing exoneration of the 'Stockwell Six' after a 50-year wait for justice. From the CCRC I at least managed to obtain reports on the 1995 appeals. It seemed that I had reached a dead end. However, I know that I had not stolen any money from the clients' or office accounts, and that it was an issue constructed entirely by Nichols. Why am I led to this conclusion? Apart from what is set out later, I came to realise that I was a victim. When this was pointed out to me, I was somewhat sceptical, but having researched the issue, I now believe that the diagnosis was absolutely right. But I had to get on with my life. I applied for a few warehouse / packing jobs, and stuck with them while I studied for a further degree and then filled a few lecturing posts. I was, and still am, determined to have my conviction overturned. It is difficult to live with the fact that I had been convicted of a serious crime and had spent time in jail. Everything I had achieved in the past had been wiped away. It is not just a case of doing time then going back to square one; the stain is there forever. The Rehabilitation of Offenders' Act 1974 bars me from a job that I came to love, returning to the law as a solicitor. I could never shed the past as somewhere it will be recorded in the various media outlets, principally on the WWW; some people will always know what you had been convicted of, friends and family.

As I said, one has to start all over again. I had not finished with the CCRC and having spoken to Edd King, a good friend of mine also a lawyer, he thought that, in view of the legislation the CCRC have to abide by, there were possibly other routes to pursue. It was not that the CCRC were unhelpful; on the contrary they did spend time on responding to my approaches but to a great extent their hands were tied. Their response was as follows.

'The CCRC has looked at your conviction before under reference ..... /2001. On 17 July the CCRC decided that your case should not be sent for a new appeal. We enclose a copy of the statement of reasons that we sent you on that date.
Documents.
The surviving documentary record of your case is very limited. In your application you say that you have no paperwork relating to the case and during the first review we made enquiries with the Crown Prosecution Service, the Court Service and the Devon and Cornwall Constabulary. We were advised that these files had been destroyed in accordance with normal retention policies and the Court of Appeal has not retained any paperwork. Apart from the statement of reasons that accompanies this decision notice, the only documentation that we have retained from our first review is the case record.
Your application grounds.
You have submitted a 14-page document setting out your submissions in detail. The following summary is a lightly-edited version of your own summary which appears on page 11 of your application form:
1. You were not shown any prosecution statements.
2. There was no 'paper trail'

3. You were not fit to give evidence and you did not
4. The prosecution took three weeks to present their evidence
5. You believe your defence team were incompetent
6. There is substantial new evidence about the integrity of the main prosecution witness. [See back of book re. prosecution; says a lot about Nichols.]

You suggested that the following individuals / organisations could now assist:
1. Pope and Brooks [former partners of the firm]
2. Trial solicitors
3. Counsel
4. The Law Society who may have been involved at some stage*.

*I suggested that the firm may have made a claim on the SIF to recover the alleged losses to clients; see below.

The CCRC's powers to refer.
The CCRC may refer your conviction to the court if:
1. there is a real possibility that your conviction would be overturned if it were referred and
2. this real possibility arises from evidence or argument which was not put forward at your trial or appeal [or there are exceptional circumstances; [*NB exceptional circumstances to allow us to refer a case without something new are extremely rare*] and
3. you have already appealed or applied for leave to appeal against conviction [or there are exceptional circumstances; *NB1; exceptional circumstances to allow us to refer a case where there has not been an earlier appeal are very rare. There has to be a good reason why there has been no appeal and why there cannot*

be an appeal now without the CCRS's help.] [Does not apply in my case]

Summary of referral Powers of the CCRC.
Under S. nine to twelve of the Criminal Appeal Act 1995 [The Act] where a person has been convicted on indictment or by a magistrate's court in England, Wales and Northern Island, the Commission may at any time refer the resulting conviction, verdict finding or sentence to the Court of Appeal, Crown Court or County Court as appropriate.
Conditions for making of references. [Retrieved from legislation.gov.uk 4 July 2021]

[1] A reference of a conviction, verdict, finding or sentence shall not be made under any of sections 9 to [F112B] unless –

[a] the Commission consider that there is a real possibility that the conviction, verdict, finding or sentence would not be upheld were the reference to be made,

[b] the Commission also considers —

[i] in the case of a conviction, verdict or finding, because of an argument, or evidence, not raised in the proceedings which led to it or on any appeal or application for leave to appeal against it, or

[ii] in the case of a sentence, because of an argument on a point of law, or information, not so raised, and

[c] an appeal against the conviction, verdict, finding or sentence has been determined or leave to appeal against it has been refused.

[2] Nothing in subsection [1][b][i] or [c] shall prevent the making of a reference if it appears to the Commission that there are exceptional circumstances which justify making it. By S. thirteen of The Act a reference shall not be made unless the Commission consider there is a real possibility that the conviction verdict or finding or sentence would not be upheld were the reference to be made. Where [1] potential exceptional circumstances are apparent and [2] where there are no potential exceptional circumstances but a real possibility is apparent.

1. If there are potential exceptional circumstances, the case will be reviewed by a Case Review Manager. That review will be limited to issues directly associated with the potential exceptional circumstances. Once that review is complete, the case will proceed through the normal decision making process. The issue of exceptional circumstances will be kept under consideration throughout the CCRC's review of the case and at the decision making stage.

2. A real possibility may be apparent on the face of the application without there being any identifiable exceptional circumstances. In these circumstances, the applicant will be advised in writing to apply for leave to appeal, even if the usual time limit for such application has expired. Where appropriate, the applicant will be advised to seek legal advice.

My comment.

From the above and the report, I conclude that there is still scope for the CCRC to intervene in my case, and in particular on information which is set out later, and which raise questions as to the claims made by Nichols, the competence of my legal team, the failure of the CPS to requisition documents from Nichols and which were in existence at the material time and which would clearly indicate that there was no case to answer, that the so-called 'schedule' of offences, by which it must be assumed related to payments out of the client account was in fact and could only have been copied from my own client card from my sale proceeds, and that my barrister should have established that the 'auditor' should have carried out a forensic account of all the above documents and not used second-hand or copied or edited versions or in any other respect not supported by evidence. He like any other prosecution witness had legal a duty to the produce evidence in his possession and which may help the defence. I had approached the CCRC on a different tack but again they refused to intervene and sent a final determination. The approach I took will be set out later in this book.

Comment on the CCRC. Edited for length; you are advised to read the whole report. [Retrieved 5 July 2021 https://insidetime.org/ccrc-too-deferential-and-lacking-rigour/.]

A report by the Westminster Commission on Miscarriages of Justice concluded that the CCRC suffers from underfunding, lack of independence and a remit which prevents it from acting over some apparently wrongful convictions. It is the last resort for people who claim to be victims of miscarriages of justice in England, Wales and Northern Ireland, and receives around 1,300 applications a year from people asking it to review their convictions or sentences. *Yet the report points out that in some recent years it has rejected more than 99% of applications,* and after years of cuts its annual budget is less than £6 million. MPs and peers on the All-Party Parliamentary Group on Miscarriages of Justice launched the Westminster Commission in 2019. Its co-chair, former Solicitor General and Conservative peer Lord Garnier QC, said: *"As the last hope for the unjustly convicted, the CCRC must remain alert to the need to be properly equipped to deal with wrongful convictions. We believe our recommendations would lead to an improvement in the CCRC's investigatory work, prevent it from being too wary of the Court of Appeal, and allow it to maintain its independence."*

Responding to the report, the CCRC said: "We are pleased that the Commission recognises some of the excellent work conducted by the CCRC, but we also take seriously those areas where improvements are said to be needed. The CCRC will give detailed consideration to the Commission's recommendations, taking the opportunity to learn from the Commission's inquiry and to implement any changes which we believe will improve the CCRC and its work." It said it supported the idea of the Law Commission carrying out a review of the "real possibility" test, and was committed to improving its communication with applicants. It has asked the Ministry of Justice for extra funding.

The Fight Goes On.

My next port of call was the Law Society. The first contact was in February 2020 when I explained that the firm operated for a number of years from three offices amd since ceased business. The partners were Nichols, Pope and Brooks, and, at the material time, me, the writer. From information received from the CCRC, I have reason to believe that sometime in 1995 or very shortly thereafter, the firm made a claim on their insurance in the sum of £90,000 [ninety thousand pounds] or thereabouts. This claim arose as a result of my [alleged] misconduct. The claim they made, or which I believe they may have made, was fraudulent in that the alleged losses were a total fabrication. Unfortunately, prosecution files have been destroyed, but hopefully you have retained details of any claim the firm made [by the principal Nichols] and one assumes would include the findings of any forensic accountants who may have undertaken work on the case and who copied you into their findings. I am happy to let you have the information I sent to the CCRC and their response. I can outline the tenor of my suspicions about the case by means of a brief discussion when you can ask any security questions to establish my bona-fides. Alternatively, if you furnish me with an email address I will pass on the issues I think you should consider.

I am not seeking to obtain any information to which I am not entitled, but I would like the opportunity to set out my reasons for doubting the validity of any insurance claim, indeed about the whole case, and supply the names of other persons who could, I believe, be approached. Should you suspect that a fraud has been perpetrated, and that this should be investigated, I am perfectly happy to support your department in whatever action it deems necessary. At the very least you could respond to this letter as suggested above. I can be contacted on email .... and by 'phone on ....

They replied, 'I'm sorry for the delay in responding to your below email. Your email was passed to my team to review our records and provide you with a response. I can confirm that our records in regard to a firm's client accounts [which would be SRA accountant reports or COFAs declaration they are satisfied that the firm is managing its client account in accordance with SRA rules] are retained for 6 years and then destroyed in line with the SRA's record retention schedule. Therefore, we are not able to assist you further re. this matter. Kind regards. Information Governance Officer Solicitors Regulation Authority.

I was then referred by Investigations and Supervision, Solicitors Regulation Authority to the Solicitors' Indemnity Fund and that in 1999 the profession elected to move towards an insurance-based open market scheme with the consequence that the Solicitor Indemnity Fund [SIF] entered into run-off with effect from 1 September 2000. I then made contact and spoke to a George R.............. of the LS insurers, and on asking about claimants he gave me a number of names of [former] clients who he believed had claimed or on whose behalf claims were made over the period I was with the firm, September 1988 to August 1991 or thereabouts when I left. Only one of the names was known to me, being the daughter of the developer George [Kate] and for whom I never acted and never met. Developer George's wife was called Sheena. The names I managed to note during the conversation were: Avery, Baker, UCB Group, Capital Headlands, Rev. Brown, Alexander, Gibb, Abbey National, Brittain / Britain? and Lighter. None of them could have been my clients, as I never had any claims made by during my time with the firm. UCB Group, Capital Headlands, Rev. Brown and Abbey National were most definitely not my clients, and the other names mean nothing to me.

A further response dated October 2020 from George R.............. of the LS insurers, 'I write further to the recent information you have provided to me on 8 September 2020. I am sorry for the delay in responding to you, however I have now reviewed all of the information that you have provided. I understand that you were a partner of the firm between 26/04/1989 and 28/08/1991 and that during your time at the firm an individual named Nichols raised some serious allegations about you. Your report states that you were alleged to have gotten into financial difficulties and in order to alleviate the difficulties you transferred money from the firm and the client's accounts into your own account or for your own use to pay private debts. You have informed us that he blames you for £90k missing from the accounts over the period 1989 to 1991. I have read the document that you have provided and I am aware that you disagree with the allegations made about you. You have provided your reasons as to why the allegations are untrue. I understand that in order to investigate this matter further you have asked to see the firm's SRA files to see if there are any anomalies in the annual accounts which you believe do not support the allegations. Unfortunately, we cannot provide this information to you due to the passage of time which has passed. You have raised concerns about an incident that occurred almost 30 years ago and in view of this we no longer have the documents that you have requested. I have decided to close this file with no further action, we do not have enough evidence to instigate this file further, and given the length of time that has passed, it is unlikely that we would be able to retrieve such evidence. Thank you for the information you have provided. Please note that the information relating to this matter will be retained on our records. As with all reports that are made to us, they can be looked at again in the future if similar instances arise.

My comment.

In view of the names mentioned above, it seems some information was retained. This looks like another dead-end, but at least I now know what happened to the firm; it ceased trading on 31 December 1996 and split into other firms, one run by Nichols the other by Pope. Nichols ceased trading in July 1998 and amalgamated with another firm, W, whose principal referred to my former senior partner as *'Keyhole Nichols'*. Pope ceased trading on 5th January 1998 and the successor practice is E. I managed to contact Pope's later employer and he passed on a note addressed to Pope to see if he would contact me. He did not. I tried on two further occasions at both of the properties at which he was the registered proprietor, but he failed to respond. See later for copies of those letters and my comments re his failing to respond. Nichols apparently took a post with a local firm of solicitors specialising as an expert in dealing with motorcycle accidents, but that job lasted for a very short time, either because he failed to bring in the work, or more likely because Nichols was a very poor employee in many respects I could highlight.

The Senior Partner

I sent a note to Pope. It was dated 15 June 2020

Dear Charles,

Firstly I hope this letter has landed 'on target'. It concerns a mutual acquaintance, Nichols, and I would very much like to discuss a number of matters which have recently arisen regarding that person and the old firm. Understandably, I am unable to go into any more detail, but I hope you will regard as personal and confidential but will be happy to discuss once contact has been made. I can be contacted on email at on ………………………….. or by 'phone ………..……………….. I trust you will treat this as 'pressing'.

Thank you, etc.

    I can only assume that he did receive the note, but for reasons known only to him he failed to respond. I also tracked down the defence barrister, but his 'phone was answered by someone who would not give an email address as she was concerned that my approach may be some kind of 'scam'. In the event, I sent a statement of my concerns about the case, and asking if he would contact me. He did not. Nor did he respond to approaches made by the CCRC. Again, I am sure he must have reasons but it would have been courteous if he could have at least acknowledged the communication and that he had no intention of becoming involved, if indeed he felt that way. I also had a conversation with Irwin Mitchell regarding a possible negligence claim against my solicitors, but was way out of time. The next port of call was the police regarding a question of withholding evidence, but I ultimately preferred to not pursue Nichols or Pope directly but go for a judicial outcome.

CCRC – Again.

Bearing in mind that the initial approaches to appeal [by my barrister] were based on capacity, time and misdirection, I now sought to approach the CCRC on different aspects of the case.

5TH November 2020

<u>FAO: Rachel Ellis [Commissioner]</u>

Dear Commissioner,

I refer to my correspondence of May this year and now write with regard to the recent concern expressed by Helen P............, Chair CCRC, on the delay in bringing criminal cases to trial. Article 6 of the ECHR entitles a person charged with a criminal offence to a 'fair and public hearing within a reasonable time by an independent and impartial tribunal'. 'Reasonable' is not defined, but must be interpreted according to the facts of every case. It is significant that the majority of convention violations are excessive delays, in breach of the 'reasonable time' requirement in court proceedings. There can, for example, be no justification in bringing a case to trial after a 42 month delay.

In my case it was in August or September of 1991 when the principal of my firm, 'the senior partner' accused me of being a 'tea leaf', his actual words. One must assume that at that time he had passed to the police who conducted their first interview in

September 1991. Within a week of my leaving that firm and working as a locum, he had informed my agency of his accusations, and I was therefore unable to continue working. Sometime considerable prior to this accusation being made, Nichols had embarked on a somewhat bizarre campaign of behaviour towards me which was intimidating to say the least, and led to my GP diagnosing stress and depression well before I departed from that firm. I believe that this 'theft charge' was a continuation of that behaviour. It is all set out in a statement I have recently prepared, and which I am happy to forward to you if you so request and which sets out all the various matters which require to be aired.

For the next three and a half years I was unemployed, receiving medication for severe and prolonged migraines and depression which necessitated a brain-scan, and spent virtually the entire period at home with occasional visits to the local magistrates court until the case was remanded to the Crown Court for a hearing which took place in January / February of 1995. That is a when I had three young children, a mortgage, and no job.

My point is this; whatever the circumstances of *any* case, apart from deliberate delaying tactics by the accused, there can be no reasonable hope for a defendant to properly respond to the prosecution's case after delays such as I experienced in bringing my case to court. I can think of no reason why the case should have taken so long to be listed. Further, the case took three weeks to present, and over that time I doubt if I took on board more than ten percent of the proceedings. To leave any accused for that period of time is cruel in the extreme, whatever his personal circumstances, and I do not believe that any judge has the right to ignore the ECHR provisions. Further, the Judge [now deceased] placed me on the 'self-harm' register after conviction so must have had good reason for doing so, which supports my contention as to my demeanour at the material time. My view is that the delay was occasioned by Nichols, primarily, and possibly, but unlikely, by the inefficiency of the CPS. The time delay apart, I am certain that had I been able and fit to present my case, I would have been found not guilty. This contention is supported by documents I have in my possession, but I want you to concentrate on the delay in bringing to trial.

What would I have raised at my trial? Not once did I see any documents on which the case against me was based. *I only knew of the sum allegedly taken by me [£90k] when I received the information from you earlier this year.* Indeed, had my own client account card been available it would show the sum of £130,000 was paid in on the sale of my property in 1991, and all the separate payments made out of that account. The sale was managed by the Firm. The reason it was NOT available, I believe, was because Nichols used the various transactions on my card to support his claim that I had extracted funds from other clients' accounts. He also knew that had my card been available for the defence to see he would have had no case. I would also have established from the Law Society whether over the period 1989 / 91 the practice accounts showed any client losses, and if money had been lost over that period how were those 'losses' dealt with in the accounts when the accounts were passed by the Law Society over that period. Had the accounts not been passed, then I as a partner would have had informed. Am I saying that Nichols manufactured the case against me? Yes I am and I believe him to be perfectly capable of doing so.

You also stated you were *dealing with an appeal* as late as 2001, why was I not involved, or even informed of any hearings? At least I would then have been able to see all the documents relating to the case, most now apparently destroyed. The only appeal I knowingly made was in 1995. Even after all this time, it is difficult for me to commit all this to paper as I feel an acute sense of shame and embarrassment over the whole business, but I am encouraged that you at CCRC still have some paperwork relating to the case, and that SRA still have some details of the insurance claims [information provided by George R.................... of SRA] when he read out the names of some clients who had apparently 'lost' funds over the period in question, and who claimed on the SIF; but they were not my clients.

This is however not relevant to the main point in my contacting you, but just to illustrate that there were issues to be addressed. A retrial would now be all but impossible. The delay was destructive of any opportunity I had to defend myself; my case was not heard, and I told my barrister that I could not take the stand as I would not have done myself justice after which the barrister commented to the effect that *'The prosecution would tear you to pieces'*. In my state he was very probably right.   Under the circumstances I do not believe a fair trial was possible, but I do recall that the clerk assigned to my case tried to persuade me to plead guilty which I refused to do. The accusations laid against me came as a shock. Training as a lawyer was hard work, then having that career 'on the rocks' particularly when I knew that the charges were unfounded, had a massively debilitating effect.

Other issues raised by you, via the clerk, was that 'I was making notes throughout the trial'; I was not; I did not even have a pen. Secondly that the medication I was on was a 'normal dose; may be it was, but medicines affect people in different ways. That the clerk also suggested my demeanour was *'normal for people undergoing a trial'*; people are different; the clerk did not know me, and in any event he was unqualified to make such a remark.

I have served my sentence; having the case overturned or whatever one does in this situation will give me back my self-respect, allow me to continue with my legal career, but will not ever remove from my mind the time I spent in jail. I trust you will regard this as a worthwhile case to revisit, and if you so require I can forward my full statement of the circumstances surrounding my time with the firm, a statement I more recently prepared for the SRA / SIF and which I am sure you will find illuminating.

Thank you.

Their reply, January 2021.

Dear Mr Cairns, Re: your closed application to the CCRC. Your letter of 5 November 2020 has been passed to me to consider. You may recall that I wrote to you on 20 May 2020 in response to your last letter about your case. As I explained at that time, we decided to close your case in February 2020 because a meaningful review of your conviction was simply not possible. In my letter, I indicated that it was open to you to reapply to the CCRC in the event that you located significant new evidence and/or material with which we could undertake a meaningful review of your case. This remains the position. A reapplication to the CCRC must usually contain something new which has not been looked at before. In your recent letter you discuss the delay in bringing your case to trial. I note that in our Statement of Reasons on your first application to us [our ref: ..../2001], a copy of which was enclosed with our Decision Notice dated 3 February 2020, we said the following:

Prejudice caused by the delay in bringing the matter to trial. This argument was raised prior to the commencement of the trial and is not therefore new. The Commission is therefore unable to investigate this matter any further. This therefore appears to be something that we [and in fact the Crown Court] have already looked at. You should also bear in mind that any re-application to the CCRC would still likely need to overcome the fact that we could not find any contemporaneous material relating to your case. Finally, in our previous correspondence we did not say that you had an appeal in 2001. We were referring to the application that your barrister made to the CCRC which concluded in July 2002. I hope this clarifies matters. Your case remains closed.

Yours sincerely, Mr J.......... L.............. Case Review Manager.

I have to agree that delay is not a dead-cert get out of jail ticket to overturning a conviction. On delay generally, where there has been substantial delay in bringing a prosecution, the court may stay the case as an abuse of process. A stay of proceedings on the ground of unjustifiable delay will only be granted by the courts in exceptional circumstances. It will be very rare for a case to be stayed *where there is no fault on the part of the prosecution.* [my italics]; if the prosecution were not chasing the accuser over the period of forty-two months, what were they doing about it? It is an extraordinary period and as I have said a few times, in 1991/2 every piece of paperwork relating to my time at the firm was readily available. However, to establish abuse of process based on delay, *the defendant will need to prove that, because of the delay, he will suffer such serious prejudice that a fair trial cannot be held.* Even where delay was unjustifiable, a permanent stay should be the exception rather than the rule. In considering whether there is likely to be prejudice, the court should consider:-

1. The power of the judge to regulate whether evidence is admissible and
2. The fact that during the trial, factual issues relating to delay can be placed before the jury as part of the evidence and
3. The power of the judge to direct the jury about delay before they consider their verdict.

The European Court of Human Rights Article 6[1] gives the defendant the right to be tried 'within a reasonable time'. When a court considers whether there has been a breach of the right to a trial within a reasonable time, they will consider the length of the delay, the reason for the delay, whether the right was asserted [i.e. whether there were complaints about the delay] and *whether there has been any prejudice to the defendant. NB: in my case an earlier trial date may have made the discovery of documents easier to achieve [1] and [2] the stress engendered in waiting for 42 months may have seriously affected my ability to appreciate the charges and requisition documents through my defence team.*

The House of Lords has held that a breach of the reasonable time requirement in Article 6[1] should not automatically lead to a stay of proceedings. The right of a criminal defendant is to a hearing and there is no support in the Convention or case law for the contention that there should be no hearing of a criminal charge once a reasonable time has passed and a stay would never be an appropriate remedy if any lesser remedy, such as a declaration, a reduction in sentence or an award of damages, would adequately satisfy the defendant's Convention right nor would it be appropriate to stay the proceedings unless there could no longer be a fair trial or it was for any compelling reason unfair to try the defendant and finally, for the purposes of Article 6, the relevant period would begin when a defendant was formally charged or served with a summons. An interview [or arrest] would not normally mark the beginning of 'a reasonable time'.

Well, that deals with the delay issue. Or does it? The legal maxim is surrounded by caveats, as above, but whatever the reasons apart from the defence deliberately delaying, account should be taken of the effect on the defendant. Ergo, it should be considered applying the known effects of delay on the ordinary man and decisions as to whether the delay has or is likely to impair a person's ability to give a good account of himself then becomes a matter of applying humanitarian issues and common sense;

legal get-outs are just not acceptable, effectively rendering inchoate the 'reasonable time' stipulation.

See letter Times July 2022; 'Judge attacks backlog' *A judge condemned the backlog of criminal court cases as he spared a paedophile from jail. Judge Patrick Thompson said he was suspending then eight-month sentence given to Gary Shields aged 71, for possessing indecent images of children as the case had taken nearly three years to reach Chester crown court'*

See letter Times 19th July 2022; His Honour Judge Witold Pawlak condemning the already unacceptably high caseload [referring to Times [Law July 14 2022 by Mark Fenhalls, QC chairman of the Bar Council of England and Wales] 'Tackle backlog and review fees to ensure criminal bar's future']

I then decided to get Edd involved. I needed help. From now on, we were to work as a team.

The Senior Partner

PART TWO – EDD KING

I read John's submission again. I felt a great deal of empathy for him but I could not help feeling that there were a few matters which needed clarification. I called him for the answers. It seemed to me that everybody was to blame, everybody had failed him. His 'solicitor' was apparently a clerk. That was confirmed by the CCRC, and the clerk telling him to plead guilty; where did that come from? It could only have been on the barrister's instructions. Was the evidence so strong that his defence team felt they had already lost? And why was John shown none of the evidence in particularly the 'schedule' of losses? How was it that over the period from charge to trial the lawyers saw him no more than four times? Then his barrister not contacting him; I've seen the bundle he sent to the man's chambers, so that was a tick. Then the police, He once recalled his telling them they ought to do their job properly, as he had stolen nothing; their asking John what had he done with the money. At this stage in the investigation, surely the police would have been shown the evidence of theft and where the money had gone. Then the statement, *'Even if you return the money you have stolen, we will still charge you'*. The home visit from the single 'cop' who asked them if they had overseas accounts. I feel as John did, that it was a 'ploy' by Nichols who perhaps genuinely believed the bloke might come up with some valuable info; or it was just an idea for the bloke to have a snoop around for reason unknown to me. Visits by a lone cop on any investigation just does not ring true, and it was not any one of the officers [DH amd MS] who were dealing with the matter. Single visits on investigations by the police does not ring true, anyway, and John's wife confirmed the visit.

The lack of documents; at the time this all 'blew up' there were plenty of documents to be had; all John's clients' files; there would have been letters of complaint about missing funds or approaches by their lawyers; transaction slips; the clients' accounts cards; John's own card and sale file that produced £130,000.

Why did Nichols see fit to ring all the solicitors John could be working for in the town to tell the employer that John had been stealing clients' money? Obviously, John lost his job. Why the delay of 42 months before it came to trial? Was there no application to the court to ask why? Was it because Nichols needed time to forge the documents to 'prove' his allegations?
Much of this was set out in John's statement, and it all seemed feasible to me. I looked up the Bob Hare definition of a psychopath. It seemed John had it right. What I wanted was a reason for Nichols acting like that and I think too that John had it. It was a money thing. The firm's overheads were not being met by income so Nichols resorted to doing what he did. It seemed that claims were made on the insurers in 1988 to 1991; these were the dates I was interested in, but that does not mean that claims were not made prior to that. But it was hard to see how Nichols could benefit from his pursuit of John unless he claimed from the law society insurers.

Then there was the stress aspect. Stress affects every part of the human body, even causes hair loss. The stress John had to deal with in his earlier job lasted seconds, minutes maybe hours before it was dealt with. Not years. Unless you were a POW. Stress can cause short and chronic memory loss, supporting John's that he had no recall of anything that happened or was said after the first few days of his trial. It can result in Mental health problems There is a long list of factors that cause mental health problems and stress is just one of them. Understanding what causes you stress can help you to find solutions. If you can recognise the early signs that you are feeling stressed, you may be able to take action that reduces the effects of stress. Some 70% of people had felt stressed at some in their lives. So it is a problem that affects a huge proportion of the population. Stress is the degree to which you feel overwhelmed or unable to cope as a result of pressures that are unmanageable. Sometimes beneficial such as the pressure of doing something daunting motivates them to continue but there are also very negative effects of stress ...' The note continued, and it became apparent to me that I could not blame John for not acting sooner. His wife told him to forget it. He had to build a new career for the sake of the whole family, and she for one did not want the business to re-ignite the old issues of earlier. Perhaps not heeding his wife's or my doctor's entreaties to give up the job and move elsewhere just made him worse.

Even without Nichol's antics, a law firm can be a stressful place to work, the main factors which come into play are expectations, significance and certainty which together make a breeding ground for stress and bullying. Lawyers are generally high performers who have very high expectations for themselves and don't want to lose. They strive for significance and don't tolerate people who hold them up. Sometimes lawyers are blinkered to what is going on around them as they are so focused on their end-goal. They can be impatient, rude and vindictive to lawyers at other firms. But most lawyers care about their clients and colleagues. Having such a mix of people's rules and values often leads to conflict. A bully often values certainty and significance highly because of the nature of law. Lawyers need to be accurate and powerful and when people start to feel under pressure, stressed or like they are losing control, they lash out to protect themselves. In your case, you just became so focussed that you could not see where it was taking you. This is by no means a way of saying that you did wrong as regards your clients, but wrong by yourself. *You should have gone long before you did. Now with the benefit of hindsight, you damn well know it'.*

Opening A New Front.

A massive re-think on the whole business was inevitable after my long chat with Edd; appalled as he was by the behaviour of my 'senior partner', we decided to run through the whole affair, with him taking the part of Nichols and me being myself. Then we reversed rôles, and the outcome was the same in each case; I could not have done what I was supposed to have done without the alleged thefts coming to light within weeks if not days, and certainly not over a period of two years 1989 to 1991 or in the sum alleged. We both concluded that the only way it could have been done, forgetting the complicated mechanics of it, is if over the period in question there was no audit [as is required by the Law Society in order to renew the firms practicing certificate], and / or there were no internal audits at all over the same period, and by that time, we also decided, there would be serious issues with the clients, especially on the conveyancing files.

John then passed me his latest contact with the CCRC if nothing else to just keep their files open. I had noted two mistakes; he sold his house in 1991, not 1989 and the trial delay was 42 months, not 42 weeks.

Date: 12 April 2021 Mr ......, Case Review Manager.

Dear Sir,......

CCRC Ref: No. ..../2020

I appreciate that you are underfunded and overworked, but nevertheless do a difficult, essential job in looking at miscarriages of justice. Unfortunately, with our judicial system there are far too many cases which rightfully demand your services. That said, I once again refer to my earlier correspondence in the above matter, aware as I am of your previous responses but implore you not to dismiss this approach out of hand but give it due consideration. I am positive that this case should be reviewed for the reasons I set out below. The prosecution case as set out in your file is as follows: 'Between <u>1989 and 1991</u> the defendant got into <u>financial difficulties</u>, and it is alleged that in order to alleviate those difficulties he transferred money <u>from the accounts of his employers and clients to his own account</u> or for his own use to pay private debts. It was alleged that he did so dishonestly without the authority of his employer or clients. The total sum involved was some <u>£90,000.</u>'

There were eight counts of theft. I offered no evidence at my trial principally because I had no idea what was going on beyond the first two days of the trial. This is not a case of 'new evidence coming to light' which I understand is one trigger for you to take up a case; it is rather a case of available evidence not seeing the light of day at the material time. But first a few points.

1. The allegation suggests that I managed to extract some £90,000 [approximately £146,000 in today's terms] over a period of two years 1989 to 1990 and 1990 to 1991. The delay in its apparency is a first issue; the sum equates 89/91 to about £940.00 per week over the so this begs the question; how was it 'missed' until the third quarter in 1991.

2. The firm of Nichols and Pope was not a substantial enterprise by any means; my office comprised me and a part-time accounts clerk, receptionist-cum secretary all in one building.

3. My discipline was conveyancing, a process which entails every client being sent a 'completion statement' showing every penny *in* and every penny *out* and a copy of the statement as with all other correspondence is retained on every client's file. *I never had access to any of the files held in either of the other two offices; ergo, any alleged 'extractions' could only have come from my own clients and not from the clients of the other offices.* Any lawyer whose discipline is property law will know that if funds are 'diverted' on any conveyancing job, completion of the transaction fails and the consequences would be immediate and dramatic. All my transactions went through to successful completions.

4. As regards the employer's office account or accounts; to suggest that it was ever able to sustain 'losses' or even half of them on the scale alleged is beyond parody. I have good reasons for saying this. From time to time office and clients' accounts were

subject to periodical audits, and certainly more often than bi-annually.

5. Despite the allegations, the partnership accounts were all passed by the Law Society during my tenure, but when I joined the firm their accounts for the previous accounting period were, according to Mr Pope not passed, so they needed a fresh practicing certificate held by someone who was not employed by the firm over the period in question; I, and unbeknown to me at the time, conveniently filled that requirement.

6. The date 1991 is significant because that was the year [in August] when the firm completed my house-sale, a matter the senior partner agreed to take on for me. It is perfectly normal for any partner / employee of any solicitor's firm to instruct his firm to take on that kind of business. On completion, the sale proceeds of £130,000 or thereabouts were paid into my client account; the only reason for me having an account in the first place was because of my house sale.

7. I was never in 'financial difficulties' as alleged. I had income from a number of businesses and sold on/about 1986 to 1989. My wife and I were 'comfortably off'. In addition, I made healthy profits on my numerous house-moves. I have retained for family history purposes details of all my business interests, property sales and purchases.

8. Nichols initiated 'proceedings' against me ca. September 1991 and at that time there was available; [a] <u>My own client card</u> [which

was removed by Nichols to his office with a balance of around £11,000] and [b] <u>All my clients' account cards and client files</u>.

9. Reflecting on the above issue, *any of those documents* would have shown that the allegations were unsustainable but, notwithstanding their availability in 1991, it still took over three years to bring the matter to trial, and the above documents were not then produced to me or at the trial; indeed, had they been available to the CPS at the material time, the case could not have proceeded.

10. In or around 1991, the backlog of criminal trials at was measured in months, not years. If no delays were attributable to the CPS, then why was there a 42 month delay in bringing the matter to trial.

Anybody who has any knowledge of solicitors' client and office accounts and of conveyancing in particular will immediately recognise that the case does not hold water. My belief, and knowing the man as I do, is that he fabricated the evidence against me. That is a matter for him to live with and on which you have to take a view based on my earlier submissions. But what I am suggesting is that there are questions about the safety of the conviction. Even if you knew *nothing else* about this appalling business, and even after such a lengthy delay, the above facts on their own are sufficient to raise serious doubts and I should at the very least have the opportunity of putting them to the test; the weaknesses in this case lie totally within the wording of the allegations. I hope you can appreciate that there are issues that should be explored, and to that end I look forward to your response. I am sorry that I have to refer this matter to you once again, but I feel very strongly that persistence is the key to seeing justice done.

Thank you. ……………………………..

   Their reply.

16 April 2021 12:48 Subject: CCRC Ref: No. ………./ 2020

Dear Mr ………………, Please could you confirm your current address for our records. Kind regards, Casework Administration ,Criminal Cases Review Commission

REPLY Sent from Mail for Windows 10

My current address is ………………………….. ………………….; I do not think you ever had any previous address. However, please do NOT send any correspondence to me regarding this matter, but always use this e-mail address. I hope this request means that you are not ignoring my latest plea for some inquiry into the matter.

Thank you. ………………………….

19 April 2021 Dear Mr ………………, Your application to the CCRC.

   Thank you for your CCRC application. We have given your case a reference: ……………../2021. You will need to tell us this reference whenever you contact us.

COVID-19: The CCRC is continuing to work on cases. However, the on-going pandemic is likely to continue to cause some delays. Please bear with us in these difficult circumstances. We will provide you with a further update before the end of July 2021. If you want to contact us in the meantime, please email info@ccrc.gov.uk. It is important that we know everything that you think went wrong with your case before we look at it. If there is anything you have not told us about your case you must tell us now. If you do not tell us something before we start our review of your case we might not look at it. When we write to you, we will not normally send copies of our letters to anyone else unless you contact us and ask us to. You must tell us if you change your address. What happens next? The first thing we will do is look at your case to see whether you have already tried to appeal directly to the Court.

• If you have not tried to appeal directly to the Court, we will look at your case to see whether there might be any "exceptional circumstances" [very special reasons] why we should investigate your case, even though you could still try to appeal directly to the Court. For more information on exceptional circumstances, please read the enclosed leaflet.

• If you have appealed or you have had an application for an appeal refused, we will look at your case to see whether it raises anything new and important. ["New" means something that was not raised at trial, or on appeal or in an earlier application to the CCRC.] We will also be looking to see whether we need any more information or material to help us assess your case. This stage of the process takes around 3 months. We will write to you again before the end of July 2021 to give you an update. If you have not appealed, or your case does not raise anything new and important, the next letter we send might be the CCRC's decision on your case. Yours sincerely, Casework Administration Criminal Cases Review Commission

The CCRC has looked at your conviction before under our references ...../2001 and ...../2020. On both occasions, although for different reasons, the CCRC decided that your case should not be sent for a new appeal. We enclose a copy of the CCRC's statement of reasons for each of those reviews. As we observed in the statement of reasons for your second application, the surviving documentary record of your case is very limited. We said, ultimately, the fact that neither the summing-up nor the Court of Appeal judgment have survived means that a meaningful review of your conviction is not now possible. That remains the case. We have, nevertheless, read the points that you have made in your letter to the CCRC dated 12 April 2021. They can be summarised as follows:

1. You ask how a loss as large as the loss alleged in your case could have been missed until the third quarter in 1991.

2. You observe that the firm was small. The office where you were located comprised yourself, a part-time accounts clerk, a receptionist and a secretary.

3. You say that if funds are diverted on any conveyancing job, the consequences would be immediate and dramatic. All your transactions were completed successfully.

The Senior Partner

4. You say that the suggestion that the office accounts could sustain losses on the scale alleged, is beyond parody. The accounts were audited more than bi-annually.

5. The partnership accounts were all passed by the Law Society during your tenure.

6. Your house sale in 1989 [actually it was 1991] was dealt with by the firm. The proceeds of about £130,000 were paid into your client account.

7. You were never in financial difficulties as alleged.

8. In September 1991, when Mr Nichols initiated 'proceedings' against you, your own client card, and your clients' account cards and files, were available. Any of those documents would have shown that the allegations were unsustainable, but they were not produced to you or at the trial.

9. You ask why there was a 42-week [month actually] delay in bringing the matter to trial.

10. You believe that Mr Nichols fabricated the evidence against you. It appears to us that even if we were not prevented, by the lack of papers, from conducting a meaningful review of your conviction, these submissions would potentially be vulnerable to the objection that they raise matters that ought to have been raised at trial [if they were not raised at trial]. We appreciate that the difficulty caused by the lack of papers must be deeply frustrating

to you, but we have to deal with the situation as it is, and not as we would like it to be.

We have thought about whether there is anything else that we could investigate, but we have decided that there is nothing that we could investigate that would make a difference to your case or to the decisions that we have already made. This means we do not think that further investigations by the CCRC will make any difference to the decisions that we have already made in your case.

Your case is therefore closed.

Notes

1. The CCRC has a legal duty to disclose any new material it has obtained during its review which would help the applicant make their best case for a reference to the appeal court. The CCRC may, in its discretion, provide other material where it considers it appropriate.

2. The material may be sent to the applicant in its original form, or as an extract or it may be summarised.

3. In this case, the CCRC has not sent you any material other than this letter, and the Statements of Reasons from the two previous reviews, because the information is adequately summarised in those documents, or in material already available to you. Your papers If there are any documents or letters you have sent to us in connection with this application that you would like us to return to you, you must contact us within 3 months. The CCRC will

destroy any paper files 3 months after case closure. Electronic files are retained for a minimum of 5 years in accordance with the published retention schedule, available on our website.

The CCRC then set out again *in extenso* the law the CCRC has to follow when looking at my case.

John replied.

As you must understand, I am deeply upset at your decision not to take up the matter. It seems I have been condemned by procedural issues, effluxion of time and the victim of a thoroughly dishonest and unpleasant character. However, I shall nevertheless pursue my case on the issues I set out in this application. The case against me as outlined in the charges just do not add up, whatever may have taken place during the trial. And I believe I was badly let down by my own defence team who just did not ask the right questions. I wonder what counsel and Pope would have said if they had bothered to reply?

Thank you anyway for the time you have taken on this.

They acknowledged.

Thank you for your email. Whilst we are sorry to read that you are disappointed with our decision on your application, that decision was final. There is no right of appeal against a decision of the CCRC but you can:

- make a complaint to the CCRC's Customer Service Manager if you think you have not been treated fairly.

- seek judicial review of the CCRC's decision if you think that there was something wrong with the way we reached our decision.
- make a further re-application to the CCRC in the event that you locate any relevant material that we could review <u>and</u> have something new and significant for us to consider.

We hope this information is useful to you. Your case remains closed. Kind regards, Casework Administration

My comment.

If raised at trial, the case would not have proceeded to a prosecution; if raised before trial, it would not have gone to trial. I was disappointed with the decision, but it was what I had expected. Edd was expecting a similar result. What was his game plan?

PART THREE – JOHN CAIRNS AND EDD KING

When One Door Closes.

I wanted to point out to John an issue he may not have considered too closely, one he alluded to in his brief. It is this. I have written it so you can go through it line by line. Here." I handed him a typewritten sheet.

'The sum allegedly stolen was £90,000 over a period 1889 to 1991. That period would actually cover three accounting periods. actually three years, so it is even more extraordinary that the accountants did not discover the alleged theft over that period. However, if we used say mid-1989 to August 1991, it is just a little over two years so your earlier calculation was more or less right. I have used two full years just to simplify the maths, but we must both bear in mind that it represents monthly sums possibly in excess of that figure, some less. Even over three full years it represents £2,500 per month. You also state that the accounts over that period were passed without the question by LS as they also told you. Even if you were looking at just a few months, at the sums above, £3750 or £2,500 it would have raised accounts issues with any auditor, let alone a full twelve months, £45,000 or £30,000 depending on the period used. Further, it is unlikely that Nichols covered any losses, or that his accountants / auditors provided false information. And, had you or anybody been extracting that kind of cash it would have been immediately obvious, like within a month, especially on any conveyancing transactions.

The Senior Partner

From what you said about the office account, it could not in any event have been pillaged to the levels above, or at all and here I bear in mind the odd £7,000 transfer to the office account from the £11,000 on your card when Nichols took it. That was undoubtedly to cover an overdraft.

The date when all this 'blew-up' viz., August 1991, is clearly significant. If as you believe, Nichols used your £90k as the sum allegedly stolen, that could only have been in August 1991 when you completed your sale, and when Nichols took your client card, which, as his firm did the conveyancing, would have shown your transactions. If Nichols had however, genuinely lost that sum through theft, it would have been immediately obvious, firstly, and secondly could have been from if not one client, then just a few over a period of weeks or even a full month. And there would have been no accounts issues with the LS. Also, the clients from whose accounts the money was stolen would have been immediately available to testify against you.' However, no clients gave evidence as you recall.

I surmise therefore that Nichols cooked up this whole business based entirely on your use of your own funds, and as you have already stated, this was when you received the 'odd' 'phone calls re. client account overdrawn and the mysterious £7,000. It was all smoke and mirrors.

<u>I conclude therefore that the prosecution case was based entirely on fiction, and Nichols and very probably Pope have committed very serious offences.</u>

John looked very close to tears, and I was not surprised.

"Now, John, as I mentioned a while ago, we still have to plough through the other questions, to get down to the mechanics of the business, as per the discussion and rôle play we plan to do. Let's look at the investigation process. The police arrest and question, they gather evidence and take witness statements. The investigations can take a long time. In my case, you said that Nichols produced evidence such as a list of monies you had allegedly stolen, and it may have appeared to be an open and shut case. But I doubt whether the officers assigned to the case questioned Nichols about any of the matters we discussed above. Then when the police have the information and completed their investigation, the case is passed to the CPS who decide whether to charge the suspect."

"Yeah. I do recall that whenever I met with the police officers, they were telling me that Nichols made a bit of a nuisance of himself asking them frequently whether I had been charged, and secondly, the cops asking me what I did with the money from which I assume that the records Nichols showed them did not lead to any source they could determine. Or were too lazy to determine or attempt to do so. And never asked to see my bank statements, so exactly what they did investigate, I fail to see. Maybe it was a deliberate ploy by Nichols because he didn't want to have any checks done which would raise questions as to his evidence, I just do not know. And I also doubt that once the matter was with the CPS that it took them over three years to bring the case to trial. Something was going on."

"It is the CPS who advise the police on cases for possible prosecution, then review cases submitted by the police for prosecution. I wonder just what 'review' they did. They determine the charge and prepare cases for court and present those cases at court. I also doubt that the CPS would be concerned about looking at the solicitors' accounts process and whether any of the considerations re the same were ever looked at. It appears to fail from the word Go."

"That's as maybe, but I was charged anyway with theft. The sum allegedly stolen was £90,000. What does that say?"

"It's a lot of money to steal in eight hits."

"Explain."

"It means that on each occasion I was supposed to have lifted money from the clients' accounts or from the office account, I made off with about ten thousand pounds. Let's be charitable about this. Suppose I lifted the same amount in forty hits, each hit would equate to just over two thousand pounds, and even that's a lot of money, in today's figures that's about three thousand four hundred ish. The firms office account might not have had that amount in it, and could well have been running on an overdraft."

"But it could possibly have been taken from the clients' accounts?"

"Very probably, yes, but subject to a few caveats."

"So?"

"There are many caveats, and no doubt I will touch on them as we continue. As my work was ninety-percent conveyancing, and that on average a conveyancing file would be open for about six weeks, the client would soon be asking a few questions, like, what was this two grand for? He would most certainly ask if it was anything like ten grand."

"Whatever it was, how would he know you had slipped the money out of his account?"

"Every penny in and every penny out appears on the client's card …"

"But you could put it into your account …"

"I could, but the cheque would be made payable to the firm, and if I had asked the client to make the cheque payable to me it would have raised problems because the client could get that cheque back showing my name and really chuck the shit into the fan."

"Or you could have paid it into your own account in your office."

"Yes, I could. Then it would show up on my card so when the client asked about his cheque, he would see it had been paid into the firm's account but there are two problems. You could never put a cheque from, say Mr Deacon, into the account of Mr Westbrook and get away with it because the cheque amount and payer would be entered onto the card. That's the bookkeeper's job."

"You could have been paid in cash."

"Could have, but you know as well as I do that as solicitors we can only accept up to £500 in cash, a relatively small sum, as per the various MLDs … money laundering directives …"

"John, I doubt that if you were the guy who was into nicking loadsa dosh, the Law Society accounts rules regarding how much cash you can accept from a client would not be of too much concern to you."

"Possibly not. Anyway, he might ask for a receipt … the client would also know what our fees would be and before the sale and purchase are completed we'd send a completion statement telling the client what he'd have to find. Essentially any shortfall on the net funds released on his sale and the amount of any mortgage he'd applied for was the sum he'd have to find in order to complete. Every item is listed. He would know roughly the figure well before his sale anyway, and that is the amount he would have to send to me in order to complete the transactions. You know well what such a statement would show. And this is not for your benefit but for the readers only."

The Senior Partner

Completion statement

		Debit £	Credit £
To:	Purchase price	243,000.00	
By:	Halifax Gross mortgage advance		182,250.00
To:	Mortgage advance deductions	30.00	
By:	Shared Equity		48,600.00
By:	You on account		191.36
By:	Reservation Deposit		500.00
By:	You on account		11,650.00
To:	SDLT @ 1%	2,430.00	
To:	Land Registry Fee on transfer	270.00	
To:	Costs purchase	495.00	
To:	VAT on our costs	99.00	
To:	Costs Help to Buy	150.00	
To:	VAT thereon	30.00	
To:	Costs SDLT	50.00	
To:	VAT thereon	10.00	
To:	Costs Local Search	12.50	
To:	VAT thereon	2.50	
To:	Electronic ID check inc. VAT	2.68	
To:	LR fees & Bankruptcy search fees	18.00	
To:	Developer's document fee	144.00	
To:	Bank Transfer fee inc. VAT	36.00	
By:	Balance from you to complete	3,588.32	
		246,779.68	**246,779.68**

Total disbursements inc. VAT   £3,615.66

[This is from a recent conveyance as an example]

115

"Now, you tell me where you can slip in a few thousand quid for John Cairns?"

"So what if he saw that the deal was going to cost him an extra two thousand pounds? What would you say?"

"I'd have no answer. If I had made a genuine mistake, I would have to explain it in detail, and if it seriously inconvenienced him very possibly come to some accommodation regarding the fees. Every statement would in any event be marked *'Errors and Omissions excepted'* and if he moaned I'd refer him to the head office. Two grand is a lot of money … enough to recarpet a small house."

"What if it wasn't a conveyance. What if it was a trust or executorship matter?"

"You mean where a substantial amount of money was held in our account over a longish period with no or with very little contact with the clients?"

"Exactly."

"Firstly, I did no probate work over my time in the office, and if indeed the firm was doing any trust work I would not have handled it. I assume the head office would do all trust work. However, Edd, I really never knew what went on in the head office, or what Nichols did there. Further, trust funds would doubtless have been held in a separate account. And I had no access to any clients' cards apart from my own clients, and only my clients' files."

"You know, Edd, this is the conversation I should have had with my defence team. However, and bearing in mind my note about the clerk who had conduct of my case, though I suspect my barrister was the guy who first mooted the idea, trying to get me to plead guilty, that guy Nichols must have done a really good job on stitching me up. However, because I was really in the dark."

"I know what you're going to say ... that because you only saw your defence solicitor about four times, and didn't even see this schedule of alleged offences, and that you were sitting on your arse for forty-two months gradually seeing your life fall apart brick by brick, how the hell were you supposed to act normally? I'm not blaming you for that John, look at the statistics. And I believe that you had a brain scan because of your headaches ... did they think you had a brain tumour?"

"That was the reason for the scan. Now about the caveats. As you know, every year solicitors have to have their accounts passed by the Law Society in order to have their practicing certificates renewed. No PC, no work. It's easy. You already know about my sudden promotion to partner. Nichols says that over the period 1989 to 1991, two years, I nicked £90,000. Yet, he submitted accounts to the LS over the periods 1989 to 1990 and 1990 to 1991..."

"How do you know that?"

"Easy. The firm retained it's PC. So, how does he ratify his [false] contention that, on the one hand there was according to Nichols an ever-increasing amount of cash being removed from the client [and office] accounts, yet the firm managed to retain its practicing certificate? And don't forget, it must have been apparent to his auditor, hence my scepticism about him or her. If the auditor had indeed been entirely independent and familiar with solicitors' accounts, which of course he should be, it would have taken only minutes before he realised something was seriously wrong. And if there had been issues with the accounts, the LS would have told me and the other partners. It's SOP. Ask yourself, how did he do that if he was £90,000 down on the client's account? Again, let's be charitable and assume half came from the clients and half from his office account. Is he saying, in fact it's exactly what he's saying, that neither he nor his auditors noticed until August of 1991 or thereabouts that about £90,000 had been extracted from the clients' accounts from 1989 onwards? And why is the date 1989 so significant? When I sold my property, the sale dealt with by his conveyancing team in his other satellite office, he knew I was selling because I asked him if he, or rather his firm, would deal with it. He stated correctly that I could not deal with it myself, so a file was opened in that office. Every file has its own client card. I had mine. On completion of the sale, £130,000 or thereabouts went onto my card. That sum less disbursements remained on my card to deal with as I thought fit."

"And as you have already said, at the time of sale, your new place was virtually complete. So, what if you then removed all the money to your private bank account? I mean closed the card?"

"Good point. The protocol as regards keeping clients' files varies between three and five years or thereabouts. And it applies to whomsoever the client is, even in this case, a partner of the firm or an employee. So, if indeed I had taken out all the money, but bear in mind the £11,000 balance, Nichols would have been only too keen to show that transaction, knowing full well that any sums subsequently taken from the clients' or office accounts and applied for my benefit could not have been my own money my £11,000 or so excepted. Ergo, it would have been nicked. So when this former builder of mine stood up in court and said he was '*surprised to have been paid with a client account cheque*' two points arise. Firstly, had Nichols produced all the necessary paperwork to establish that all my money had already been withdrawn from the clients' account, the builder would have had a valid point. However, had he shown my client account to the court it would have shown that the builder's cheque was paid from the sale proceeds of my property, so he clearly could not show the card as it would have destroyed that particular aspect of the prosecution case."

"So, why didn't your defence team ask to see the card? Or mention the account issue? Or, if indeed you had taken out all your money in 1991, all he had to do was prove it by requisitioning your bank account records to show it. And that would obviously have been done in or around the time the cops got involved."

"Right, as that would have proved conclusively that any money subsequently taken for my benefit was nicked but that still does not square with the accounts being passed if he had been telling the truth. That £90k or whatever must have been a legitimate series of payments made in such a way as to not arouse any suspicions, to not set alarm bells ringing, to not have clients calling about stolen cash, so it must have been from my own card on legitimately authorised payments subject of course to my seeing what they were. There can be no other explanation as to how Nichols cruised along for two years while alleging that £90,000 was taken by me. Another point. Bearing in mind that I sold my property in 1991, if as Nichols alleges, I or anybody had been milking the clients' accounts over period 1989 1990 It would have shown up, obviously. However, what if there had not been any accounts issues. The accounts would have been passed by the LS over those years. It therefore looks very much as though Nichols invented figures 1989 to 1990, and just used my own client account card to find the sum of £90k which I obviously had in my account. But I don't know why my defence team didn't ask to see the card. But card and accounts apart, other matters arose which made me believe that they were utterly incompetent, solicitor and barrister alike. I have no idea how they worked together, but one or other of them seemed very keen to get me to plead guilty. You know, I think I am ... was ... entitled to assume that the persons trusted with my business knew what they were doing. It is not my place to ring them and ask whether they have done this or done that. However, as history now shows, my trust in them was 100% misplaced."

"You were right about that!"

"Yes. I can only imagine that as Nichols had over three years to work on collecting and very probably fabricating evidence to support his case, he did such a good job that my team was overwhelmed. Another point, and this is a substantial one, why didn't I see any of the prosecution statements? Why was I not shown the schedule that the CCRC mentioned? I might possibly be being unfair here, because it is worth mentioning that counsel might have planned to submit a good argument in my case, but from what went on prior to the trial, in effect nothing, I doubt that he had any good arguments. Nobody ever said to me, *'what about this?'* or *'what about that?'* or *'how do you explain this?'* and on reflection, they didn't seem to be really interested in the outcome, and further, I do not think they had the ammunition to fire at the prosecutors."

"So, what would you have done?"

"Okay. Going on what I said above, and looking again at the charges. And bear in mind here, I had absolutely no idea what on earth the prosecution were going to throw at me. My lawyers though must have known. Look at the prosecution case as I discovered them from the CCRC, viz.,

'... that between 1989 and 1991 I got myself into financial difficulties, and it is alleged that in order to alleviate my financial difficulties I transferred money from the accounts of my employers and clients to my own account or for my own use to pay private debts. It was alleged that I did so dishonestly without the authority of my employer or clients. The total sum involved was alleged to be some £90,000'."

"Now this raises a number of points which need investigation and which your lawyers should have asked.

Q. It implies that you had your own account. Was this an account with the firm or are they talking about some other account?"

A; It was an account with the firm opened for the sale of my house."

Q. What debts are they referring to? Did you have any 'private debts'?"

A. We had no private debts as he called it. We were building our new house, fully financed. In fact, we did not really have to sell our old property, but keeping another property for whatever reason is frankly a burden but by the time we sold our old house in 1991 the new house was virtually finished. If there had been some suggestion that we were stealing money before our sale, then it would be a simple matter for my lawyers to see my and my wife's bank statements which would show that the project was well financed and the source of the funds."

Q. Do you, or does Nichols know, the clients from whom this money was allegedly stolen?"

A. I don't; nor do I think any client money was stolen at least not by me and unfortunately I did not see this 'schedule' of payments which I suspect was merely a list of payments I had quite legitimately made from my own funds. I cannot recall what the payments were … some to the builder, some to suppliers, some probably into my private account. In any event, the new house was finished within a month of the property sale. The only list I ever saw was the one the Law Society insurer G………….. R ……………… read out to me."

Q. Were you in financial difficulties?"

A. No. I've shown you details of my various businesses sold and the property I bought and sold and all that money went into the new house. However, the jury might but wrongly, take judicial notice of the fact that people who are having houses built for them are always short of cash ... I don't think that follows, but you do see the damage it might have done to my case."

Q. I do. Nichols is saying that you were stealing money from 1989 to 1991. That is about two years. Is the date of any significance to you?"

A. Not really. It was as I said above. 1991 was when my sale went through. I think he lifted info from my card and attributed it to other clients cards to show 'thefts'."

Q. To your knowledge, did any of your clients contact Nichols to complain that you had taken money from them?"

A. No."

Q. Did any of the firm's clients contact Nichols to complain that you had taken money from them?"

A. Not to my knowledge. And if they had the first thing would have been for Nichols to contact me."

Q. Were you at any time between 1989 and 1991 when you left the firm contacted by the Law Society to say that the firm's accounts had not been passed?"

A. No. Which, if what Nichols was alleging were true, is very odd indeed."

Q. Why would it be odd?"

A. Because if the sum of anything like £90,000 or even £9,000 was missing from the clients' accounts, the annual accounts would not be passed, the firm closed down and all partners separately informed. We've exhausted this point anyway."

Q. Do you know why or how Nichols got round that little difficulty?"

A. No I don't. He could not get round it and I don't believe he even had to. It would be possible I suppose that if there had been a client loss he could have covered it himself to make everything look kosher, but firstly I cannot imagine him doing that, and there would be serious consequences if he did that, and it would be a fraud on the LS. And as the auditors are or are meant to be totally independent they would very probably spot it anyway. And as for covering the sum of £90,000 it's just impossible to do. Anyway, there had been no thefts on that or any scale. The whole theft thing was invented by him."

Q. Why would he do that?"

A. I have no idea except perhaps he wanted to get rid of me and make it as painful as possible for me in the process."

Q. Thank you. That's extreme behaviour, very hard to understand. But in view of what you said earlier about his antics, it does ring true. Apart from the above, what other information do you think the jury should have been party to in the trial?"

A. I think they should have been told just how solicitors' accounts work, the office processes and in particular the annual accounts which all firms have to submit in order to retain their practicing certificates. It would then be up to Nichols to explain how he managed to have his accounts passed when, as he alleges, substantial sums were missing over a period of two years 1989/90 and 1990/91, the final sum being he states, £90,000."

Q. What are or were the office processes as regards accounts?"

A. Every client had his own card, and in my office all kept in a box in the accounts' office. As soon as a file was opened for a client, a card was also opened and filed with his or her details, the type of job, i.e., divorce, sale & purchase or whatever. Where not a legal aid matter, we would ask for a deposit against disbursements and when paid that would be entered on the file. So say a client dropped into the office with his cheque, that cheque would be taken to the office where I or the bookkeeper if she happened to be in would complete a transaction slip as follows; Client: Hart. Mrs A B Deposit £50.00'. The card would then be taken from the file and client details added, Deposit £50.00 Cheque number 456 Barclays. The transaction slip would he added to the others in a drawer or onto a clip as usual. If we took any money from a client's account, we would again raise a transaction slip e.g., 'Stevens D R deposit on purchase Barley Crescent £25,000 chq. payable to

Wick, Smithers and the firm cheque number. Again, the card would be annotated then the slip would be filed."

Q. How much of that would you do?"

A. I would generally complete the slip. Everything else would be done by the bookkeeper. I never wrote on any of the cards. If I wanted the cheque it would generally be completed by her and I would sign it either that day or the following day."

Q. So why was it important to have the cards in your office if the bookkeeper did all the writing up?"

A. Because I needed to see if the client had the funds available. Formerly, it meant calling another office, asking whoever answered the 'phone to check, then sending a DX to that office ... you know the score."

Q. The allegations were that you transferred funds from the clients' accounts to your own account. How would you do that?"

A. I could write a transaction slip asking the bookkeeper to transfer say, £1,000 from the Hart card to the Cairns card. It would not happen. And if I insisted somebody would be told. And if it did happen, the card would show the payment on the Hart card to Cairns, and on the Cairns card transfer from Hart to Cairns. And it would be picked up by the auditors if it ever happened."

Q. But what would happen if you just wrote on your own card a deposit of, say, £5,000?"

A. I could do that, but we'd need a payer - I could say me - and mode, e.g., cash / cheque and a paying-in slip showing that payment into the account. Each pay-in is noted on the paying-in book, listed on the back. That idea would not stand up to scrutiny for more than about five minutes, especially as I could not show where it came from and large dollops of cash lying around solicitors' offices are just no-no's and any legal accounts person would know that."

Q. But you could hand in a slip asking for a cheque from Mr Client payable to Brickies Builders' Merchants."

A. Yes, I could. But then Mr Client would like to know why he was suddenly down on the money he needed to complete his purchase, and why he was paying a business about which he knew nothing. All the firm would have to do is contact the payee and ask on whose behalf it was paid. That would all be discovered within weeks, certainly a month or so."

Q. But what about cases where the funds sat on a file for probably years like probate or trust work where any unauthorised extractions would not come to light for ages?"

A. We've already been there. I did no probate or trust work. I don't know who in the firm did."

Q. What do you perceive as the weaknesses in Nichols' accusations and your defence team's performance?"

A. Nichols.

1. The LS accounts being passed over the period.
2. The sum alleged so large that the firm could not function with such a loss.
3. My clients' cases could not have all completed satisfactorily as they did if I had been extracting such vast amounts from their cards.
4. That I had no access to clients' cards from the other two offices so I could obviously not write out cheques on the other offices' clients' accounts.
5. The time it apparently took Nichols to 'discover' the alleged losses.

B. My team.

1. Not one of the above points were raised by them. Had even one been considered, it would have released the tsunami of other weak points in the prosecution. In fact, I'm surprised that the CPS didn't pick up on a few of them. Any solicitor, and I mean solicitor, not barrister, not a clerk, would have immediately seen the problems with the Nichols argument. Also, it would have taken only an hour or so to run through the accounting procedures and the LS annual PC renewal process for the jury to see right through the prosecution case. However, with a clerk who may or may not have by then passed his solicitors' account exam, the weakness in Nichols's argument may not have occurred to him. Clearly, it did not occur to the barrister either, and I wonder just how they just took all the evidence at face value, without question. It was the stuff they saw that I did not see, unfortunately, and had I, and had

I also been my old self, I would have ripped it to shreds. In conclusion, I was patently very badly served in this appalling case."

Q. If you could ask Nichols just one question what would it be?"

A. Did you, Mr Nichols, claim on the Solicitors' insurance to make up the alleged loss to the clients?"

Q. Why that?"

A. If he knows that the whole thing is once more under the microscope, he knows that if he said 'yes' to having made claims, then he could face charges brought by the LS; if he says 'no' then the next question is, how if at all, were the losses repaid. If it were a genuine case then a claim would doubtless have been made. And every claim would as a matter of course be investigated by the insurers' staff. Or do the insurers pay out on a conviction? However, my view is that he did not, as the LS insurers would have asked all the questions we have been through above. And they would surely have concluded that as the alleged losses commenced as Nichols claimed in 1989 Nichols would have had to answer a few very awkward questions. And may well have his claim rejected. If he claimed and was paid, then no doubt the payments went into the firms' account. Nichols must have been pretty smart in the way he presented the evidence, and in the way he avoided presenting all the relevant documents but just as bad was the way my defence team failed to spot the obvious. He was also taking a very big risk, as, if his ruse were exposed in court, he would let's say, have been very embarrassed. However, I think the

Achilles heel in this case is the wording of the charge. Firstly, as it did with me once I heard all this from the CCRC, it would jump out of the page at any solicitor who knew the first thing about accounts, and secondly he would be demanding to see my client card, the cards of those Nichols alleged had lost money, all the relevant cheques and transaction slips. Remember, all this came up before the end of 1991, and there is every reason to suppose that those papers were then available, and if they could not be produced, then reasons why not. Further, who drafted the 'schedule' we have heard about? Was it the same 'accountant' who removed my card? Or was it the man who turned up at my house accusing me of having numerous overseas accounts? As we said in the beginning, *'the story just does not add up'*."

Q. How can you remember all this stuff, John?

A. Edd, I can remember things back to the time I used to go to the loo on my own as a kid. I can remember the names of people I was at junior and secondary school with, particularly the girls. I can remember the registration numbers of the cars I owned from my first back in 1964."

"Okay. A final word on this?"

"Yes, two, actually. I do not think Nichols allegations that I was stealing money period 1989 to 1991 is actually sustainable, because he must have known that he could not have 'covered it up' 1989 to 1991 if it were true. But he knew that the sum alleged did pass through my own account due to the house sale. But if he just claimed that that sum was stolen since my card was opened in July 1991 [even though no funds went into that account until early 1991] he would have to state that I managed to steal £90k *within a couple of weeks* which it patent nonsense. So he therefore *retrospectively* claimed it to be over several years. Remember, *nothing happened in this business until he took my card to his head office* which gave him all the ammunition he wanted to make up the allegations!"

"That seems to make sense, John!"

"And two. Even though all this business happened many years ago, and as there is no statute of limitations on crime, and Nichols did commit a crime or crimes in dealing with this case, he should be pursued. All I want is to have the conviction set aside so I can even at this stage in my life recover the working years I lost. I imagine I would have been in a far better position had this business not been dreamt up by my persecutor!"

Q. Now, you said that you contacted Pope again. What did you say to him and what was the response."

A. I wrote to both addresses I got for him. I know his wife's full name and the land registry confirmed those addresses. I attach a copy of the letters I sent."

Q. What was the point of the letters?"

A. I did not believe that he would be part of this business, so I wrote asking him for his views, but he failed to respond, so I am left with the impression that he must have known what was going on. Regrettably, I must assume he is as guilty as Nichols."

Q. Who else did you contact?"

A. I tried three firms of solicitors including the firm who acted for me. None wanted to know. I also tried to contact the police officers who dealt with the case and two other police forces. None of them were interested.

"Thank you John."

The letters to Pope.

Date 28 June 2022.

RE: Donald Nichols

I doubt you will exactly welcome this letter but be that as it may, I hope you will respond. I send a letter to your other address but if you did receive it, I received no acknowledgement. It is my intention to appeal the case brought by Nichols and I believe you can help. It is fortunate there is no statute of limitations on the offence of perverting the course of justice.

Whereas I recognise that Nichols was not admired for his work ethic, and doubtless you found his assumed title of 'senior partner' galling as you and he were equal partners. Whatever deprivations you and other staff suffered under his regime they did not come close to the hardships I and my family suffered due to the dishonesty of that man. You may have wanted on occasions to jump ship but your investment in the business probably prevented that. It was a shame as I believe you and Mr Howard are both decent men who deserved better.

Nichols is dishonest, a bully, serial liar and a sociopath. Such talent is commonly found within law firms, but rarely taken to Nichols extremes. You must know the ridiculous defence he dreamt up to wriggle out of his 2007 drink-driving conviction; a concoction of lies, an imagined female lover whom he 'gallantly' refused to name to protect her marriage and job.

The firm Nichols & Pope closed on 31 December 1996 and split into other firms, Nichols, which ceased trading on 29 July 1998, and Pope which ceased trading after thirteen months. The fact of the short life of your new enterprise probably caused you even more heartache. Nichols had no 'family', apart from the imagined police-officer girlfriend, one of many with whom he apparently enjoyed 'intimate relations'; I wonder what happened to 'Sue ....', his 1988 girlfriend.

Bearing in mind Nichols' earlier career, acting corporal throughout his five years in uniform, it would be odd if he as a policeman, of sorts, had not shared with you his 'suspicions' about me, but I doubt he did. My property sale file, accounts card, my clients' account cards, cheques, transaction slips and bank statements, all available at the material time, viz., from October 1991, all prove the allegations to be false.

Had you an inkling of what Nichols was up to, you would have put a stop to it. You were kind enough to keep me informed on other matters, such as when Nichols unilaterally appointed me as a partner five / six months after I joined the firm as the accounts had not been signed off by the Law Society. I never was flavour of the month with that man, in fact I would suggest our relationship was toxic, so promotion was not an act of altruism on his part but a necessity. Being a partner would have made me, with certain caveats, jointly and severally liable for the practice debts if not otherwise settled, so it was little wonder that Nichols took an unnatural interest in my personal finances. Later you told me about your wife …………….. helping out at the ………………… office and which led to your being accused of trying to 'take over the office'. My wife, a trained and experienced legal secretary, helped out when Nichols engaged a replacement for D………. . She was untrained but with my wife's help we managed. Nichols wanted a 'cheap' replacement, indicative of the parlous state of the office account hence my having to replace the only electric typewriter with a PC as soon as I moved in, on the tacit but grudging approval by Nichols that I would in due course recover the expense together with the cost of a make-over for the office.

To cut to the chase; the charges I faced carried fatal flaws.

'Between 1989 and 1991 the defendant got into financial difficulties, and it is alleged that in order to alleviate those difficulties he transferred money from the accounts of his employers and clients to his own account or for his own use to pay private debts. It was alleged that he did so dishonestly without the authority of his employer or clients. The total sum involved was some £90,000.'

I only discovered the £90,000 'theft' when I contacted the CCRC not many years ago [I was undertaking some non-related research] and to say I was shocked by the figure would be an understatement.

I was 'experiencing financial difficulties. I was never in financial difficulties; I had started a number of businesses in 1977 after leaving the forces, and my wife and I enjoyed a decent lifestyle, and on the birth of my daughter I let my ……………. property and moved into a new-build at ……………… in ……… and started to offload the businesses. A year later, we sold the ………………..home and purchased another property [……………………..] and in 1988 began building a new house [………………….]. I still have all paperwork relating to my property portfolio and the other businesses. The last property sale, in August 1991 [marketed at £130,000 and which I had bought for £65,000] was managed by your conveyancer and net proceeds paid into my account with the firm. Prior to my 1991 sale, I had no client card. I moved into my new house in mid-August 1991.

Consider the £90k Nichols said I stole from my clients; let's break it down; in early August the net sale proceeds were entered onto my own card held at ……………..... I apparently managed to spend £90k between sale in August and my leaving you at the end of the year, but Nichols came up with a 'schedule' of payments to cover 1989 to 1991. When my card was removed from the ……………… office it held an £11,000 balance. However, as stated above, I had no card until the house [………………...] was sold.

To suggest that anybody could have removed what amounted to £3,750 per month for 2 or three years is laughable for several reasons; one; a firm as small as yours, and certainly the ………… office, could not bear such losses for more than a month or so *without it coming to light and if there were genuine losses there would have been queues of clients outside the office; two; I had no access to either the …………..or the ……………….. files; three; the accounts were audited [1988 to 1989, 1989 to 1990 and 1990 to 1991] but didn't highlight any anomalies; fourthly; 90% of my work was conveyancing and my cases went through without a hitch all evidenced by the usual completion statements and I received no complaints from my clients; fifthly; to suggest anybody could have taken anything from the office account is beyond parody.*

When Nichols' 'accountant' removed my card to his office with a balance of just over £11,000, a series of weird allegations arose. Firstly, a call saying that the client account was overdrawn [oddly, nothing more was heard] but it fits in with Nichols' little 'plot'; then the 'mysterious' payment of £7,000 into his office account. He telephoned me to ask if I had paid that money into his account, ridiculous as that was, but I believe he called me in case I later demanded my money [£11,000] and he could then point to the 'mysterious' transfer' alleging some 'mistake' and maybe agree to repay in instalments, if at all. Then his serving me with a County Court summons claiming £3,500. I entered a defence, but nothing more was heard, and I believe that Nichols just helped himself to the £3,500 balance on my card.

The totals viz., sale disbursements, my spending, the £7,000 and the £3,500 came suspiciously close to the net sale proceeds of my sale.

It all points to a protracted campaign by Nichols to discredit me for reasons known only to himself, but which I am confident was based on generating a smoke-screen to cover the practice's financial ills. Little wonder that he did not produce records of all my personal and client transactions.

It never entered my mind what Nichols was up to. I had always believed it was something to do with the LS accounts rules. Naïve? Maybe, but bear in mind it was 42 months before the matter came to trial and that over the period I was unemployed, on medication, with young children. In the opinion of my law professor, many 'open goals' were missed by the defence, unfortunately facilitated by Nichols withholding that evidence and my being too ill to give evidence.

I am contacting you as I believe you can help with this matter which is now with the CCRC et al. I hope you won't feel imposed upon. I have fuller statements one of 16 pages and one of 120, but rather than overwhelm you with verbiage, I would be obliged if you can ponder a few points. It is hard to believe that Nichols managed to keep the whole imagined affair from the partners, but maybe not, bearing in mind the man's character; I believe that one moniker attached to him is 'keyhole Nichols'. He had also been banned from a few local pubs in view of his somewhat robust comments which verged on the offensive.

There is much more to this, but more salient points are set out here. What he did to his business and yours was caused by his downright dishonesty, engendered by a need to prop up the firm, but I don't suppose it mattered to him how he achieved that, legally or illegally.

Points for you to ponder.

1. What was the issue with the legal executive from ……………..
whom I replaced? By the remarks left in his diary he was clearly
very unhappy. Was he also a Nichols victim?

2. What was the issue which had Tim S…………. accounts clerk,
removed from his job?

3. Did Nichols really want to employ me, or just keen to close the
Tiverton office? …

4. … or was I employed just so my Practicing Certificate could be
used to allow the practice to continue working until accounts
issues 1987 to 1988 were resolved?

5. Why was he so 'anti' ……...? Was it that he could not afford to
keep her? Didn't he have the guts to just ask her to go instead of
running her down and insulting her at every opportunity?

6. What did you think when Nichols and you visited the
…………….. office, just a few days after I moved in, and his asking
me to 'understate my salary to the agency'. [………………..]?
Was it because the practice was short of cash?

7. Did Nichols recover or try to recover the 'lost' £90k from PI
insurance? It would have been odd if he didn't. If he did, one has
to ask, where did that money go?

8. Was the turnover ever sufficient to ensure the comfortable
running of the practice?

9. If Nichols wanted me gone, why didn't he just ask me to leave
instead of his coming into the office on occasions asking, 'How do
I get rid of a partner?' and then engaging in those damaging

allegations? He may have made it clear to you in .... that he wanted me gone.

10. Why was he, even in the early days, ringing the office two or three times per day to ask the girls what I was doing, and had I sent out any bills? Accounts issues? Cash-flow problems?

11. David .... [your one-time office clerk] admitted he was sent by Nichols to .... 'to spy on me'; did you know that?

12. Do you recall the 'meeting' at .... when Nichols opened the proceedings with 'I didn't know we had a tea-leaf in the firm' ? And the references to my builder? Clearly, resolving issues was not on Nichols' agenda. I assume you know that he then 'phoned my new employer with damaging allegations which obviously meant I could not stay in that job.

13. And when one evening in October you drove up to see me to ask me 'Are you holding onto or controlling client's money', were you sent by Nichols, or were you alarmed by the allegations he had been peddling around the office and came up of your own volition? You clearly had not been asked by Nichols to make that visit.

14. When did Nichols inform you of a £90k 'loss'? I assume it was very shortly after he had obtained my card.

I expect other incidents will occur to you, and if they do I would be happy to hear them if relevant to my campaign to overturn the injustice visited on me. I doubt you or anybody else engaged with Nichols had a bumpy-free ride, but were probably subjected to periodic vilifications for a few more than the three years I was employed.

Perhaps it might be productive if we could meet on some 'neutral' ground to discuss this matter in full. I'd like to know how fate has seen you and your wife through your troubles and perhaps I can tell you what I have been up to.

Thank you in anticipation of your response, and please do bear in mind that it is my intention to have this conviction overturned, and your help would be greatly appreciated. I believe you may know of certain matters which will be very useful in my endeavours.

If you do not want to contact me directly you can email either of my advisors, viz., ………………..…….on ……………………………..or ……………………...….. on …………………………………………….. to set out how you wish for the matter to proceed.

Regards to you both.

The follow-up letter to Pope.

RE: DONALD NICHOLS

Charles, please do not ignore this letter. I am sorry that you have chosen not to respond to my earlier letters. Indeed it is remarkable if you do not feel there are issues to be addressed, as prima facia it appears that you may not be an entirely innocent bystander in the affair. I believe you are, but this view is becoming less credible in the face of your lack of response.

We do not need to make this more complicated and painful than is absolutely necessary, but your lack of response is not helpful.

The content of my missives must surely cause you to question the veracity of Nichols' claims, viz., that I somehow managed to extract nearly £4,000 per month period 1989 to 1991 without it becoming apparent. If anything like that amount had been purloined even once it would, in the normal course of things, have come to light within a month if not sooner. If indeed anybody had been stealing that amount of money over the period, then it highlights serious issues with the firm's accountants but Nichols was never that divorced from its financial agonies.

The claims are patent nonsense and I'm sure you know that, and as a decent individual you must harbour a desire to right the wrong visited on me and my family, unless of course, you have reasons for not doing so. Once the matter is again aired in court, any contention that you were unaware of, and had no hand in this appalling business might not be easy to swallow.

Difficult as it is for observers to believe that the alleged 'theft' on that scale went undetected and is therefore a fiction, it is equally hard to believe that what Nichols was up to was not a joint enterprise cooked up between you and he, and, to be frank, your silence thus far does make one lean towards that conclusion. The consensus of your being complicit is not one I wish to entertain, or that you failed to keep a check on what Nichols was up to. I don't believe he would have shared his plans with anybody. I think you can understand the difficulty we are having in reaching the same conclusion as I wish to promote, that this was a covert enterprise conducted solely by him, a person who does not conform to normal rules, business, social or otherwise.

The Senior Partner

I sometimes wonder what it was that your accounts lad Tim had done or was accused of doing which forced his removal from employment, and the circumstances of your accounts not being passed period 1987/8. Your practice was always dogged by financial issues of one sort or another, and if you can bear to revisit the travails of your firm and the treatment of employees by Mckenzie and the other points mooted in my last missive, they should be enough for anybody to question the allegations I faced. It might be that you were also a victim.

It beggars belief that the alleged losses only 'came to light' in 1991 when Nichols 'discovered' them; not your bookkeeper, accountant, auditors or any clients any one of whom would have immediately alerted you [the firm] to any discrepancy in their individual files and bearing in mind the scope of McKenzie's allegations, there would have been many of them. Logic suggests that Nichols was pursuing an ulterior motive whereby some benefit could accrue to him, even if it were to 'top up' the office account with my £7,000 as mentioned in my earlier note. Extreme it may appear but it was not beyond Nichols due to his distant relationship with decency and honesty.

The issues I raised if addressed candidly, will throw a new light on the matter which is what I intend should happen. As a former partner and innocent party, and even if my assertions cast the slightest doubt about the case, it is incumbent on you to investigate them by revisiting the case. The man has had his fun; his actions had serious consequences and caused significant delay to the administration of justice, and he must now pay the price; the matter is going to be referred to the courts and I'd rather you were a witness and not a defendant. The advantage I have is that Nichols is known to be a serial liar inter alia.

I do not know what kind of relationship you enjoy with the man but I must accept that you might alert him to this approach and that is a matter for you but either way it should not affect the honesty of your response, nor should you be bullied into dropping the case. I hope we can sort out the issues between ourselves before it becomes an embarrassing and time-consuming interruption of your otherwise peaceful retirement.

Further, I might suggest that your wife may have had serious doubts about the Nichols character; it only took my wife one meeting with the guy for her to conclude that he was a thoroughly dislikeable person, and she was not surprised at his later actions.

I am keeping conduct of this thus far because lawyers are very expensive but I am acting on best available advice. I cannot give you a current address at the moment as am on the move keeping up with my family, but that does not mean that I am beyond reach.

I appreciate you do not wish to contact me directly but you can set out your position by emailing either one or both of my advisors, viz., ……………………….. or…………………… on …………………………….. to set out how you wish for the matter to proceed.

It may be that you should pass my earlier missive to your own lawyers [maybe ……………………… with whom you used to work?] to whom I can pass copies of my earlier correspondence if you have not retained them and who will doubtless give you a robust assessment of McKenzie's actions and whether you could be vicariously liable either by acts or omissions to act as a consequence of your earlier engagement with Nichols. How you proceed could have far-reaching implications, either positive or negative, for both of us.

Thank you both and kind regards,

The wash-up.

"Right, tell me what you think about the criminal justice system bearing in mind what you've been through. You have read my little book on criminal behaviour and prison. Your thoughts please."

"Well, it's broken, as you know. In certain circumstances, adverse inferences can be drawn from a defendant's silence as set out in the Criminal Justice and Public Order Act 1994 as amended, and the inference one mostly encounters is that the guy is obviously guilty. This is understandable. We have the adversarial system in the UK and there are drawbacks and some advantages with that system. However, what I want to explore is why a defendant actually has to give evidence, and for this, I want to give you a few examples from my case, but I want to do so on the basis that my defence team had done their jobs properly, had obtained sight of all the relevant documents and had the benefit of my being asked about the points made by the prosecution.

First the builder. We know he said that he was surprised to have been paid by a client account cheque. Without any input from the defence, that is indeed a damning remark, and, perhaps rightly, the jury would tick the box actually or figuratively, as a point in favour of the prosecution. But we know that Mr Builder's evidence is questionable. We also know the prosecution case took three weeks, fifteen working days, to present. After that period, if no challenge is raised regarding the cheque, it remains a mark in favour of the prosecution. Indeed, where it might be mentioned three weeks later, will the jury go back and delete that mark in favour of the prosecution? I don't know the answer, but what I would like to happen is as follows and firstly, this is all on the hypothetical basis that as I said, had I been through the papers with my team, my barrister to then and there destroy that piece of evidence; viz.

"Thank you Mr Builder. You say you were surprised to have been paid with a client account cheque. When was that payment?"
"In 1991."
"That was er ... three and a half years ago?"
"Yes."
"Why were you 'surprised' Mr Builder?"
"Because it was clients' money, not Mr Cairns' money."
"Who told you it was not Mr Cairns' money?"
"Mr Nichols told me."
"Indeed, Mr Builder. Did Mr Nichols bother to tell you that Mr Cairns was also a client of the firm? ... Well?"
"Er ..."
"And that Mr Cairns had in his own account with the firm, a sum in excess of £100,000 being the sale proceeds of his house? Mr Cairns sacked you didn't he Mr Builder. When Mr Nichols got in touch with you he discussed this case with you didn't he? And you

agreed to testify didn't you? Do you think Mr Builder that you agreed to testify to get even with Mr Cairns for sacking you?"

And so on, so now we can see the jury transferring the tick to the defence box. Let's assume now that I still had not been through the prosecution statements. If my team had done what we suggested they should have done as above, the defence barrister could have still come up with the same response."

"Where are you going with this, John?"

"Simply that every point raised by the prosecution should be attacked there and then, not when, maybe weeks later, the defence gets it's chance to put the accused on the stand and expect him to raise these matters. It would not of course be then permitted for the defence counsel to lead the defendant if indeed the barrister had neither the capacity nor the knowledge to appreciate the issues necessary to deal with the prosecution points. The other issue with the adversarial system is that generally the best man wins. I think in my case the prosecution barrister had more to go on, was better prepared and more competent that my guy. Ergo, my guy came second. Now the second point. I do not need to labour it, but I would like to see how Nichols would react when all the business about the Law Society accounts, the list of insurance claims which I might remind you was probably only about half of those which George from the insurance company mentioned, as he started the list before I had my pen ready. Again, I contend that if my defence team had been up to the job, there would be no need for the defendant to give evidence, and maybe by his demeanour, do a crap job and effectively condemn himself. Let's put Mr Nichols in the witness box, after, no doubt the auditor had shown the 'schedule of payments' to the jury.

"Ninety thousand pounds! That's a lot of money, Mr Nichols!"
"Yes it is."
"And how much of that was from the clients and how much from the office ... can you remind us please."
"Of course. £................ from the office, and the balance £....................... from the clients' accounts."
"But nevertheless, and every credit due to you, Mr Nichols, and over the period ... er, 1989 to third quarter in 1991, you and your partners managed to struggle on with the business."
"Yes. It was hard, but we all managed."
"That was despite the fact that some of your clients had lost money from their accounts. And when did the first complaints arise, can you recall? I assume it would have been sometime late August 1991?"
"..." [*No idea what Nichols would say*]
"I see. So you as you say and despite the problems with clients' money, the firm of Nichols & Pope struggled on, you struggled on for maybe just over three years from 1989, and obviously over that period you had your practicing certificates renewed and despite the little difficulty over the period 1987/88 when your accounts were not passed by the auditors. You may recall that was when you appointed the defendant to a partnership, and not, we have heard, just because you needed a new practicing certificate to continue in business from the time he joined the firm .... If I may Your Honour, [*just once more ?*] explain to the jury the importance

of a practicing certificate ... [*He explains*] ... So you see, members of the jury, it is essential for a firm's accounts to be audited and passed by the Law Society if it is to be able to operate. [*One suspects here that Nichols is realising where this is going*] So, Mr Nichols, over the period 1989/90 and 1990/91, your accounts were passed by the law society. That is a statement, Mr Nichols, not a question. However, perhaps you could explain how your auditors managed to dig you out of the hole which you have said was dug by the defendant here stealing the very large sum of £90,000 from your clients? Let me make a few suggestions. Did the auditor not discover the shortfall in the clients' accounts? Or maybe all your clients just did not notice? Or did you pay in that amount yourself to cover it up? ... or ... and there are two other options here. The first was that there were no losses because you just invented them. Or the money you say was taken from your clients and the office account actually came from the defendant's own money from his own account paid in when your firm sold his house for £130,000. Would you like to show us that card please?"

"[*You can't find it / you never had it / or whatever*]"

"That's a pity Mr Nichols because I imagine, just imagine, that the entries on the auditor's schedule would pretty well match those on Mr Cairns' card."

"Okay, John, I think you make some very fair points. If the defence team is up to the job, there should be no need for the defendant to give evidence, as to do so might prejudice his chances of a fair trial, innocent or guilty perhaps. But the prosecution won't get the chance to question him."

"But he could take the stand. And of course the first question to him would be, 'You did steal £90,000 from the firm, didn't you Mr

Cairns?' and the reply would be, 'No I did not.' Or to bully him or to deliberately confuse him. *Res ipsa loquitur.* There's no reason why the prosecution cannot tackle the defence on their points. As I said above, let the facts speak for themselves. Once the facts are made known, whatever else is said is about this case is effectively pointless. All the relevant facts should have been assessed prior to any hearing, and all laid on the table. It was in fact here a good opportunity for my defence team to set out to the court, or before hearing, exactly what was missing from the evidence. What Nichols chose not to disclose."

Last word.

The burden of proving the guilt of the defendant lies on the prosecution who must prove the particulars of the offence beyond reasonable doubt; the jury convicts if they are sure of the defendant's guilt; the legal burden is the obligation on a party to prove a fact in issue. The prosecution normally has the legal burden of proving, beyond reasonable doubt, all elements of the offence. Whether this burden has been discharged is decided by the jury at the end of the trial, *when all the evidence has been presented*. If the prosecution has not discharged this burden, the case will fail. If a defendant has gone through the whole appeal process and believes there has been a miscarriage of justice, they can apply to have their appeal considered by the CCRC. The Commission can refer the case back to the Court of Appeal if they consider that there is a real possibility that a conviction or sentence would not be upheld. The ground for this should be that a new or newly discovered fact - fresh evidence - shows beyond reasonable doubt that there has been a miscarriage of justice. The fresh evidence must, therefore, be the ground on which the appeal succeeded and must show that the person has suffered a miscarriage of justice.

In short, at the start of the case the CPS will serve on the defendant all the evidence it wishes to rely on at trial to prove their guilt and in the event the defendant enters a not guilty plea, the CPS should disclose any other material it has and does not wish to rely on. Such material must be disclosed if it might reasonably be considered capable of undermining the case for the prosecution or of assisting the case for the accused.

Examples of this type of material include previous convictions of prosecution witnesses, statements or other evidence collected which support the defendant's account and documents which support a defendant's case. Once the CPS has made its initial disclosure, the defendant may make a defence statement which sets out the general nature of the defence and indicates matters of fact and law with which the defendant takes issue. Once provided, the CPS must review its initial disclosure of unused material and determine if there is any further unused material in its possession which, in the light of the matters raised in any defence statement, the CPS now thinks might be deemed capable of undermining the case for the Prosecution or of assisting the defendant's case.

This is all very well, and my defence team knew I was pleading not guilty. However, whether or not any material as above was served on my lawyers, it is in view of the foregoing ninety pages or so an academic point, because in any event they clearly had no idea about what evidence was then available in support of the defence. There is no point in rehearsing that argument, as whatever that evidence was my lawyers would not have realised its value even if it hit them in the face.

However, and as has been said many times in this missive, it is not a question of evidence destroyed, not a question of evidence already seen by the court and dismissed, not a question of evidence once held by the CPS and not released. It is a question of the prosecution setting out a case which patently cannot be correct because, if it were, other unimpeachable evidence comes into play which will show up the total fallibility of the defence case.

This is evidenced by two key players. The first by the defence team not addressing the obvious consequences which would flow if the prosecution case were correct and the second, by the prime-mover in all this, Nichols, either destroying or deliberately withholding information which would render the prosecution case utterly inchoate.

When you bear in mind that all the parties to this saga were lawyers, it makes one wonder just what they were doing ... or not doing. So many aspects of this case were screaming out of the pages to all parties, yet it appeared that nobody saw the obvious. Well, hopefully now this has all been aired in this little missive, somebody will agree that there has been a miscarriage of justice;

this will not rely on evidence already presented to the court; it will not rely on trawling over information withheld by the CPS; it will rely on taking a common-sense point of view which will conclude that the prosecutors were presenting which was just not possible to sustain. The competing factors do not here have to be presented by the defendant as 'his version of events' but that the evidence presented to the court by Nichols was patently false; that he failed in his duty to the court to produce all the available evidence; the CPS themselves should have seen through the evidence. This case has to be revisited.

The Future.

The CPS and the police are now, somewhat predictably, failing the criminal justice system and, disappointingly, blaming their failures on funding, but that is complete nonsense. For those of us who have been around for a while, the prosecution seems to have always had problems fulfilling its Disclosure obligations.

The Right Honourable Lord Justice Gross published a review of disclosure in criminal proceedings in September 2011 stating;

> *"Improvements in disclosure must – and can only – be prosecution led or driven. To achieve such improvements, it is essential that the Prosecution takes a grip on the case and its disclosure requirements from the very outset of the investigation.*
>
> *Of course, if the police and CPS want to support their argument that their current failings are related to funding,*

they should produce their previous representations to the Ministry of Justice that funding is affecting their ability to make disclosure and ensure fair criminal trials – but do not hold your breath waiting for disclosure of that evidence either.

In my view the only answer, following years of consistent failure, is to enforce the Disclosure Rules thoroughly by investigating each failure to ascertain whether it was an attempt to pervert the course of justice, and by making it clear in the terms of employment of both the Police and CPS, that such failures may lead to dismissal. And who was the auditor who produced 'the schedule'? Did anybody explain to the jury how solicitor' accounts worked?"

How can a guy just make a complaint to the police and dump a load of paperwork onto the CPS without either of them raising any queries? In this case there were a lot of questions to ask. But is the justice system collapsing?

Then Law Society press release 14 Jun 2019

Criminal justice system on brink of collapse - urgent intervention needed to save it.

A decade of underfunding has left the criminal justice system in a perilous state with every part of the process floundering, a new report by the Law Society of England and Wales revealed today. "The criminal justice system can touch any one of us, at any time," said Law Society president Christina Blacklaws. "Suddenly - and quite unexpectedly - we could find ourselves as defendant, victim or witness in a criminal proceeding. We rely upon the criminal justice system to ensure our rights are protected and justice is served, but it's a system that's crumbling." The report uncovers a system at breaking point. Its failures are leading to:

Injustice - *our failing criminal justice system is undermining justice in countless ways:*

- *The stringent legal aid means test is preventing many on low incomes, or in poverty, from accessing justice.*
- *Those who sit just above these modest legal aid thresholds are impacted by the 'innocence tax' – meaning someone can be found not guilty of a crime but can only claim back some of their costs at legal aid rates.*
- *Court closures are making it harder for people to access justice locally.*

Negative impact on people's lives - *our system is based on the principle people are innocent until proven guilty. Yet lives can be ruined before a case even reaches trial:*

- *"Release under investigation" means suspects and victims can be left in limbo for months waiting to know whether the police are going to pursue a case.*
- *Delays in the disclosure of evidence proving someone's innocence can have a massively detrimental impact on the life of the accused, meaning they must go through a whole legal process which would have been unnecessary if evidence had been disclosed sooner.*

- *The fact cases can be cancelled at the last minute due to 'warned' and 'floating' lists compounds this - people can emotionally prepare themselves for their case to be heard, only to find out on the day it has been delayed for another few months.*

Increasing pressures on the criminal justice system - this dire situation is likely only to get worse due to increasing pressures on the criminal justice system:

- *The average age of a criminal duty solicitor across the whole of England and Wales is now 47, and in many regions the average age is even higher. In as few as five years there could be areas of the country which have no access to a criminal duty solicitor.*
- *The reason behind the shortage is that criminal legal aid fees are extremely low and have not been increased since the 1990s.*
- *As the numbers drop, the stresses on those who remain worsen, making the role even more unattractive. This creates a vicious spiral.*

Christina Blacklaws added:

> *"Since 2011/2012, the Ministry of Justice [MoJ] has lost a quarter of its budget. This has led to significant cuts to our courts and tribunals, legal advice and representation. This is a system which is, without exaggeration, on the brink of the collapse. For victims and the accused, a journey through the system is akin to a nightmare. Unsurprisingly,*

it is those on lower and middle incomes who bear the greatest burden. A recent survey found 60% of respondents believe people on low incomes are more likely to be convicted of crimes than wealthy people. Justice and the rule of law are supposed to be core British values. If we fail to act now, we risk consigning that legacy to the history books – as thousands risk falling through the gaps. It's time to fix our ailing criminal justice system. Before it's too late."

Key recommendations:

- **Legal aid means test**: The legal aid means test must be uprated as a matter of urgency.
- **A legal aid task force**: The Ministry of Justice should procure independent analysis of the funding required to assure long-term sustainability of the criminal legal aid system. A legal aid task force should be created to evaluate any proposed changes and consider their impact on the criminal justice system.
- **Court delays**: 'warned', 'block' and 'floating' court lists should be abolished. This will avoid wasting court time, costs, and anxiety for all parties. We also recommend the Ministry of Justice considers a target deadline for youth cases to be heard.
- **Remuneration rates**: Expert lawyers must be kept within the profession to ensure knowledge and experience is retained in the system.
- **Efficiency**: The Legal Aid Agency [LAA] should review the Defence Solicitor Call Centre [DSCC]. DSCC could be replaced by an automated system, to improve efficiency

and reduce cost. We also recommend a centralised IT system be implemented for booking legal visits to prisoners, which would benefit all stakeholders.

Where are we now with Nichols?

Edd King comment.

We do not propose to let the matter drop. We feel there are some very valid issues to be addressed, and even though the CCRC might suggest that they could have been raised during the trial, it is unlikely that, had they been, the result would have been the same. Nor is it fair to suggest that the defence should have raised them; why should one be condemned by one's lawyers' incompetence. The issue is that had the case been properly investigated at the time, then these matters would have arisen as a matter of course and it is unlikely that there would even have been a prosecution.

The facts needed to revisit the case are as set out in the charge.

It certainly is not fair to condemn a man because his own lawyers were incompetent, and they clearly were, nor is it fair to discount a further appeal simply because the issues were not addressed during the trial. Neither is it as though the unaddressed points were obscure or of no consequence; the points raised in this missive but not addressed at the trial were of such weight that even an idiot in a hurry could not have missed them. And ironically perhaps, the wording of the charge would in any sensible and proficient lawyer have triggered a series of questions which the prosecution should have settled prior to trial.

Nor is it a case of documents being unavailable. The main fact on which we rely is one on which the court would take judicial note and concerns inter alia the way the law society regulates solicitors' practices. It was indeed fortunate for Nichols that his team failed to notice the obvious. However and regrettably for many thousands of other defendants, failing to address the obvious, or ignoring the obvious or for some other reason fail to meet the standards expected of them means a miscarriage of justice. Where the facts they have been given by those who instruct them, or those discovered on investigation of an offence indicate that there are other issues to address, then it is incumbent on those concerned to undertake further investigation. This did not happen in Cairns' case.

John; "The goings-on with Nichols were odd to say the least. I had worked in many firms as a locum, and I had never experienced anything like the time I had with N&P. We hope, however, to put it right.

Meeting Mr Nichols again

2007; Report 1;

Mr N.................... who tried to dodge a drink-driving rap by claiming his secret lover was at the wheel was yesterday given a 12-month ban. N.............. was chased through country lanes after a tip-off he had been boozing nearby. He led police up a mud track and fled on foot until a sniffer dog found him. But

The Senior Partner

N............... who was one and half times over the limit - claimed his senior police officer mistress was driving his car. And the court heard the man refused to identify his mistress as he feared it would wreck her marriage and career. But PC R............... T......... said he was sure there was only one person in the car. And yesterday magistrates in ……….. told ………….. they did not think his story credible. Chairwoman L….. R……….. added: "We felt there were inconsistencies, in particular regarding the protection of another." ……………….., of ………………………….. near ……………….., was also fined £700.

2007; Report 2;

Mr N .... accused of drink- driving claimed he was innocent because his girlfriend, a married senior ………………., was at the wheel. ……………………….. added that she was probably over the alcohol limit at the time. But to protect her marriage and career, he said, he could not possibly reveal her name. His claims led to speculation that someone in the higher echelons of the ………………force had been having an affair behind her husband's back and driving her lover's car while drunk. However, ……………. magistrates threw out his excuse and indicated they did not believe the woman existed outside his imagination. They convicted him of being one and a half times over the drink driving limit and banned him for a year. ……………….. was arrested after an anonymous tip-off that he was in a pub and about to drive to his isolated home three miles away in the hamlet of ……………………….

The Senior Partner

Police lay in wait and chased the car for five minutes at up to 50 mph on single-track roads. They lost it when it turned on to a mud track where their two-wheel drive patrol car could not follow.

A short while later, the car was found abandoned near .... home and a dog tracked him through a field, a farmyard and into a copse. It flushed him out and bit him when he refused to stop. Later, ... claimed he had deliberately led the police dog on a false trail, and then lied to officers about having walked home from the pub, to give his lover time to escape. *"I am a bachelor and I have a lot of lady friends who are very close,'* he said. 'I was with one that evening. I have known her since 1987 and I saw her regularly but not as regularly as I would like*. We had an intimate relationship.* I cannot name her because she is a senior member of the .... and she is married. If she had been arrested, her career in the .... would end if she was over the limit, which she may have been. "It would have devastated her marriage. She would not have been able to explain what she was doing at my place at that time of the morning. "There is nothing that would prevail on me to name her." He claimed the woman panicked when the chase started and deliberately went up the muddy lane to shake off police. However the patrol car driver, PC R............... T........ played a video of the five-minute pursuit and said he was sure there was only the driver in the vehicle. He said he had a clear view inside as it turned into side lanes and could see there was no passenger. Dog handler PC G............ R........... added that his dog .... had picked up only one scent from the driver's door and had followed it until .... was arrested. He said the dog was trained to show if there was more than one scent. PC ....

admitted the dog had been put down two months later, after savaging his sergeant during a training exercise, but said there were never any problems with his tracking. Banning .... and ordering him to pay a total of £1,064, magistrates' chairman L........ R........ told him: "We found the evidence of the police officers was credible and that of the dog handler was compelling. They corroborated each other. "We found your evidence not credible and felt there were inconsistencies, in particular regarding the protection of another's reputation. "One instance of this is that being conscious of the lady's position, you say you allowed her to drive your vehicle despite believing her to be over the limit." A spokesman for .... and .... Police said: "He was entitled to have his day in court, and it was up to him to satisfy the magistrates. "The fact that he has been convicted suggests the validity the magistrates gave to his explanation. It was a case of 'nice try but no cigar'." He added he did not believe any of the force's senior policewomen - who include an assistant chief constable - had anything to worry about.

A message from John and Edd.

If you can identify with any of the characters in this little book, whether a defendant, victim, solicitor or barrister, or somehow otherwise involved in the criminal justice system, we hope you have found this little excursion behind the scenes both interesting and educational. The main message appears to be that ignorance and lack of communication and in some cases laziness particularly by those at the point where prosecution meets defence can have serious consequences for defendants and victims alike.

Or where there are too often 'deals' struck between the two for various reasons, so the parties can move on to the next job and leaving behind a client in the cells and / or with his reputation in tatters. The Rehabilitation of Offenders' Act 1974 make it pretty certain that the defendant will never recover his life as it used to be; it is a life sentence. For persistent offenders a spell in jail is a minor inconvenience, a pause in their activities as a career criminal and in every case prison fails them and society in general.

There must be a serious, in-depth review of the use of prison as a deterrent. It does not work. It does not do what the public are paying for. It is a fraud on everybody concerned and has to change. What is the answer? We do not know and anyway, many people are paid a lot more money than we are to produce results. But what we do know is that it has to be dealt with. We are, therefore, only halfway to solving it.

September 2022

Printed in Great Britain
by Amazon